THE EVERYTHING KIDS' Gross Jokes Book

Side-splitting jokes that make your skin crawl!

Aileen Weintraub

Adams Media
Avon, Massachusetts

EDITORIAL

Publishing Director: Gary M. Krebs
Associate Managing Editor: Laura M. Daly
Associate Copy Chief: Brett Palana-Shanahan
Acquisitions Editor: Kate Burgo
Development Editor: Katie McDonough
Associate Production Editor: Casey Ebert

PRODUCTION

Director of Manufacturing: Susan Beale
Associate Director of Production: Michelle Roy Kelly
Series Designers: Colleen Cunningham, Erin Ring
Layout and Graphics: Colleen Cunningham,
    Holly Curtis, Erin Dawson, Sorae Lee
Cover Layout: Paul Beatrice, Erick DaCosta,
    Matt LeBlanc

An Everything® Series Book.
Everything® and everything.com® are registered trademarks of F+W Publications, Inc.

Published by Adams Media, an F+W Publications Company
57 Littlefield Street, Avon, MA 02322. U.S.A.
www.adamsmedia.com

ISBN: 1-59337-448-8
Printed in the United States of America.

J I H G F E D C B A

Library of Congress Cataloging-in-Publication Data
available from publisher.

This publication is designed to provide accurate and authoritative information with regard to the subject matter covered. It is sold with the understanding that the publisher is not engaged in rendering legal, accounting, or other professional advice. If legal advice or other expert assistance is required, the services of a competent professional person should be sought.

—From a *Declaration of Principles* jointly adopted by a Committee of the American Bar Association and a Committee of Publishers and Associations

Many of the designations used by manufacturers and sellers to distinguish their products are claimed as trademarks. When those designations appear in this book and Adams Media was aware of a trademark claim, the designations have been printed with initial capital letters.

Cover and interior illustrations by Kurt Dolber.
Puzzles by Beth L. Blair.

This book is available at quantity discounts for bulk purchases.
For information, call 1-800-872-5627.

See the entire Everything® series at *www.everything.com*.

DEDICATION

To my brother Neil: The slimiest person I know.
And to Aka Satchie Redstone Princess of All Things Purple, Divine, and Serendipitous
Sour Grapes, my puppy, who brings me much joy but can be pretty gross at times.

ACKNOWLEDGMENTS

I'd like to thank all the people at Adams Media who worked on this book, especially my editors, Kate Burgo and Katie McDonough. I'd also like to thank Christopher Sauer for listening to every gross joke in this book and Edward Serken for his inspiration.

Contents

Introduction

You may not realize it, but the world is a pretty gross place. Just look around. There are slimy, moldy, creepy, crawly things everywhere—even on your own body! From dust mites and hair lice to fleas and bedbugs, there are little creatures hiding in the dark corners of your home all the time! And gross gook like mold, rust, grime, and pus can appear anywhere! There's no escaping it—this stuff is always going to be a part of life. But gross things don't have to be scary; learning about them can be fun and exciting. Making jokes about them is even better.

Not only are the things around us gross, but we're pretty revolting ourselves. Our bodies do really nasty things on a daily basis, and if we're not careful, we can easily offend others with bad smells, horrific sounds, and disgusting sights. We produce earwax, snot, phlegm, and sweat every day. We can't avoid these things, so why not joke about them? This book will help you find the funny side of all the foul things around you. You'll giggle with delight reading and reciting jokes about everything from cannibals and vampires to frogs in blenders and chickens that didn't quite make it across the road. You can gross out your friends time and time again with jokes about slippery slime, curdled milk, sickening scabs, and gooey boogers. These are all important topics in the world of *grossology*—the study of grossness. By the time you're done reading this book, you'll be an expert in that field. If you love to burp, fart, pick scabs, and examine puppy puke, you'll get endless enjoyment from this book.

Getting involved in the grosser side of life takes some time and effort, so be patient. To really live the gross lifestyle, you'll have to memorize some of these grotesque jokes, pay careful attention to the freaky facts, and try every one of the gross recipes. Then you'll have to share what you've learned with everyone from your best friend to your grandmother, even if you don't think they'll appreciate it. Remember, the only thing better than being gross is being funny and gross. Spread these spine-tingling, nauseating, nasty jokes to everyone you know. Before long, the whole neighborhood will be chuckling with disgust. So, enjoy these jokes, embrace the world of creepy crud, and go forth and spread the grossness.

Creepy Critters

What did the slug say as it slipped down the sidewalk?

How slime flies.

What's the difference between an earthworm and a cookie?

An earthworm doesn't fall apart when you dunk it in milk.

Why is the letter T so important to a stick bug?

Without it, it would be a sick bug.

What do you get when you have 288 roaches crawling in your bed?

Too gross.

What is the last thing to go through a fly's mind as he crashes into a window?

His rear end.

What am I?

I can disguise myself without you ever knowing I'm there! I have no real defenses, so I have to be creative. If I'm in danger, I can pretend to be something else. When a predator comes near, I freeze and look just like a piece of wood. **What am I?**

A treehopper.

What did one maggot say to the other when they found themselves stuck in an apple?

Let's see you worm your way out of this.

What do you get if you cross a centipede with a parrot?

A walkie talkie.

What did the mother worm say to her son when he came home late?

Where in earth have you been?

Customer: *Waiter, there's a big roach in my salad!*

Waiter: *Well, stop announcing it before everyone else wants one too!*

Park Ranger: *Sir, you can't fish in this pond.*

Man: *I'm not fishing—I'm teaching my pet worm to swim.*

What did the slime say to the mold when they saw each other after a long while?

You gruesome since I saw you last.

Customer: *Waiter, waiter, what's this roach doing on my ice cream?*

Waiter: *I think it's skiing downhill.*

What did the banana say to the maggot?

You're boring me to death.

Teacher: *If I have eight flies on my desk and swat one, how many are left?*

Student: *Just one—the dead one.*

Knock Knock
Who's there?
Spider.
Spider who?
Spider everything, I still think you're pretty gross.

What am I?

I have a very unique way of hiding. First I suck the life out of a greenfly. Then I bask in the fly's juices. Whatever's left of the dead body I stick on my back to camouflage myself from predators. You could say that I'm a walking graveyard. **What am I?**

A lacewing grub.

K	E	
P	L	A

| | L | I |

Yummy!

A riddle and its answer were put into the large grid, and then cut into eight pieces. See if you can figure out where each piece goes, and write the letters in their proper places. When you have filled in the grid correctly, you will be able to read the puzzle from left to right, and top to bottom.

HINT: The black boxes stand for the spaces between words.

S	W	A
T	H	E	

	R	Y
I	B	A	L

| | W | H | A |

T		G
D	O	E

	W	
A	D	E	R

	T
O	Y?

	U	N	G
A	N	N

	A	M	E
S		A

L	L	O
	L	E

	H
C

How do you make a moth bawl?
Hit it with a fly swatter.

How did the dog train his fleas?
He started from scratch.

Sally: *Do slugs taste good?*
Mother: *Why do you ask?*
Sally: *Well, you've got one on your fork.*

What am I?

I keep a layer of gooey slime on the underside of my body so I can slither along the ground, protecting myself from any bumps in the road. This gooey substance also lets me stick to anything smooth, like your bedroom window! An outer shell protects my soft body.
What am I?

A snail.

What's the best way to prevent getting sick from biting insects?
Stop biting them.

Why do maggots eat puke?
It's a dirty job but someone's got to do it.

What did the slug say after the other slug hit him on the head?
I'll get you next slime!

What's the difference between head lice and dandruff?
Lice crunches more when you eat it.

What's the definition of a caterpillar?
A worm in a fur coat.

What did the spider do when she couldn't carry the stick on her own?
She hired an assist-ant.

What did the cowboy maggot say when he walked into a saloon?
Give me a slug of whiskey.

What was the worm doing in the cornfield?
Going in one ear and out the other.

What am I?

I lurk in dark, filthy places and I only hunt in the pitch black of night. My sharp beak-shaped mouth drills a small hole into your flesh and I feast on your blood while you sleep. I don't travel alone but in swarms. If you wake and turn on the lights I will scurry back under the mattress to strike another day.
What am I?

A bedbug.

Foul Language

Coleopterist
This is a person who has the job of researching everything there is to know about beetles. A coleopterist handles beetles all day. This way, the rest of us can learn about beetles without actually having to touch the creepy, crawly critters.

Why did the blob always stay home?
He had no place to goo.

What did the mother leech say when someone went for a swim in the pond?
Lunchtime!

Totally Twisted

Make your own slime. Mash up bananas, mushrooms, leaves, and a drop of water. Store in a sealed plastic bag for a week in a warm place. You will then have the grossest slime you've ever seen. Share your new slime bag with your friends. They'll surely appreciate it.

Knock Knock

Who's there?
Throat.
Throat who?
Throat out, there are maggots crawling all over it.

How do you keep the flies out of the kitchen?

Keep a bucket of cow poop in the living room.

Knock Knock

Who's there?
Seymour.
Seymour who?
Seymour leeches in a lake.

Stink Pinks

A stink pink is a riddle with a special kind of two-word answer—both words are one syllable long and rhyme. Of course, one of the words is gross!

What's a large vehicle that hauls garbage?
Y U C K   T R U C K

Where can you buy plastic scars and fake blood?
_ _ _ _   _ _ _ _ _

What do you call a shovel used to pick up dog doo?
_ _ _ _   _ _ _ _ _

What do you call ghost throw up?
_ _ _ _ _   _ _ _ _

What do you call an intelligent gas?
_ _ _ _ _   _ _ _ _

What's a riddle about a dead frog?
_ _ _ _ _   _ _ _ _

Ed: *I once ate a slimy slug in my pajamas.*
Fred: *Really?*
Ed: *Yes, I still don't know how he got into them.*

Why did the beetle ground his children?

They were bugging him.

Knock Knock
Who's there?
Harry.
Harry who?
Harry, scary spider crawling on you.

What am I?

I build my nests by chewing wood into tiny bits. Then I spit the wood out and mush it on the wall of your house. I make a mansion for the eggs I produce. Each egg gets its own room. When my babies hatch, I feed them chewed-up caterpillar intestines. **What am I?**

A wasp.

Knock Knock
Who's there?
I-8.
I-8 who?
I-8 a slug for lunch,
and now I don't feel so good.

How do you make a butterfly?

Flick it out of the butter dish.

How are roaches like raisins?

They both show up in your cereal.

Why didn't the fleas stick around on the dirty schoolboy?

The lice chased them away.

What did the cook do when he found a Daddy Long Legs in his meatloaf?

He turned it into a Daddy Short Legs.

What do you do with a scorpion the size of a horse?

Ride it to the hospital after it stings you.

How do you know if you have maggots in your fridge?

You'll see tunnels in the bean dip.

Why was the blob turned away from the restaurant?

No shirt, no shoes, no service.

What did one fly ask the other?

Is this stool taken?

Why do maggots like open wounds?

They don't have to fight over who gets the scab.

Why are mosquitoes so annoying at night?

They like a bite to eat before bedtime.

What am I?

I am a wiggly slimy glob that oozes. I can live in your yard, or hang out on your deck, or I can take over the whole neighborhood if you're not careful. I can be as small as a coin or as big as a table. If you try to break me apart, I just multiply and grow.

What am I?

Slime mold.

Knock Knock

Who's there?
Thistle.
Thistle who?
Thistle be the last chance for maggot pie.

What do you get if you cross a centipede with a homing pigeon?

A creepy crawler that just keeps coming back.

Foul Language

Annelid
Creepy, crawly, slimy, and *slithering* are all words that can describe annelids. They are various kinds of worms, such as earthworms and leeches.

What do you call tired bugs?
Sleepy creepies.

What do you call a bug that has worked its way to the top?
Head lice.

What's a blob's favorite drink?
Slime-ade.

What goes "Snap, crackle, pop"?
A dying firefly.

What do you get if you cross a scorpion with a rose?
I don't know, but I wouldn't try smelling it.

What kind of bugs live on the moon?
Lunar ticks.

How do fleas get around?
By itch hiking.

What lies on the ground 100 feet up in the air?
A dead centipede.

YAK YAK YA[K]

How do toilets keep in touch?

To find out, connect the numbered dots in order.
Then connect the lettered dots in order.

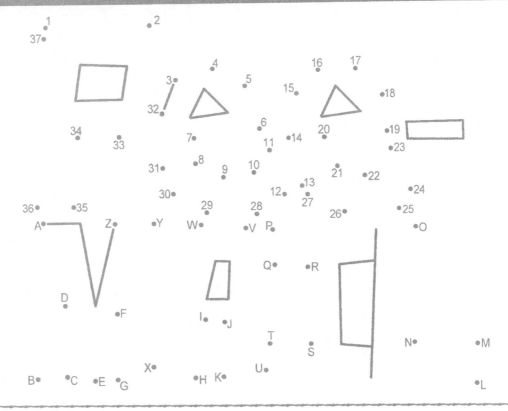

Customer: *There's a little worm in my salad!*

Waitress: *Shall I bring you a bigger one?*

Why was the mother flea so upset?

Because her children were going to the dogs.

What has fifty legs but can't walk?

Half a centipede.

Why did the mosquito get braces?

To improve his bite.

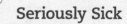

Seriously Sick

Did you ever notice that only some mosquitoes squirt blood when you squish them and others don't? This is because only females dine on your blood. A female needs your blood to feed her babies, and she lays anywhere from 100 to 500 eggs at a time.

What am I?

One of my favorite foods is rotten fruit. Give me a squishy banana left out in the sun too long, and I'll be the happiest creature you've ever seen! I've got a yellow and black jacket that makes me look pretty scary, but the truth is, I have no sting. **What am I?**

A hover fly.

Knock Knock

Who's there?
Wilfred.
Wilfred who?
Wilfred eat chocolate-covered ants?

Why are mosquitoes so annoying?

They have a way of getting under your skin.

Chapter 2

Barf-days and Other Celebrations

Boy Monster: *Did you get the heart I sent you for Valentine's Day?*

Girl Monster: *Why yes, thank you, it's still beating.*

What do you sing at a birthday party where everyone gets sick from the cake?

Happy Barf-day.

Seriously Sick

As soon as food gets to your stomach, hydrochloric acid attacks that chewed-up mush like there's no tomorrow. Acid rips apart and dissolves the food until it's ready to go through the rest of your digestive system. This acid is powerful enough to completely dissolve a stainless steel spoon, though this probably isn't your first choice for an afternoon snack!

What did the executioner say to his family?

Only fifteen chopping days till the holidays!

What's another word for bunny poop?

Easter eggs.

What happened to the snowman at the Fourth of July picnic?

They turned him into snow cones and ate him.

What do spider brides wear?

Webbing dresses.

Who did the gravediggers invite to their Halloween party?

Anyone they could dig up.

What do you get if an ax falls on your head?

Write as many answers as you can under the clues. Then, enter each letter into its numbered box in the answer grid. Work back and forth between the clues and the grid to get the answer to the riddle.

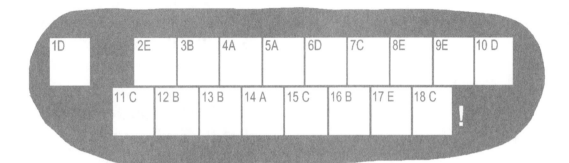

1D		2E	3B	4A	5A	6D	7C	8E	9E	10 D

11 C	12 B	13 B	14 A	15 C	16 B	17 E	18 C	

A. Top on a jar

__ __ __
4 5 14

B. Dracula's coat

__ __ __ __
16 13 3 12

C. It makes you warm

__ __ __ __
11 18 15 7

D. Kids' running game

__ __ __
6 1 10

E. Between knee and ankle

__ __ __ __
2 17 8 9

15

What do you call an insect dance?
A moth ball.

What kind of ice cream makes you barf?
Van-ill-a.

Why did the birthday girl bring toilet paper to her party?
She was a party pooper.

Cannibal 1: What gorgeous eyes you have!
Cannibal 2: Thank you, they were a birthday present.

Did you hear about the pig who started hiding garbage on Halloween?
He wanted to do his Christmas slopping early.

What shoots stuffing across the room?
A turkey fart.

How did the man feel after eating the whole Christmas goose?
He felt pretty down.

Why did the monster get fired from his job at the candy store?
He kept biting the heads off the chocolate bunnies.

Totally Twisted
Here's a fun Halloween recipe to make your very own boogers on a stick. Just mix some Cheese Whiz with a few drops of green food coloring and dip pretzel sticks in it. Serve these treats to all your friends in costumes.

Use the banana decoder to break the code and answer this riddle!

What's invisible and smells like bananas?

A	C	E
F	K	M
N	O	R
S	T	Y

17

What did the mother turkey say to her misbehaving son?

If your father were here, he'd roll over in his gravy.

Why did Mr. and Mrs. Insect cancel their vacation?

The roach motel was full.

Always Listen to Your Mother

Mommy, Mommy, are you sure this is the right way to make gingerbread cookies?

Stop talking and get back in the oven.

Mommy, Mommy, can I play with Grandpa?

No, we already dug him up three times this week.

Mommy, Mommy, I hate my brother's guts.

Well then just leave them on your plate and we'll warm them up tomorrow.

Mommy, Mommy, Daddy puked.

Hurry up and get a fork before your brother gets all the big chunks.

Mommy, Mommy, Aunt Tina bruised herself.

Be quiet and eat around it.

Mommy, Mommy, the dog is going out.

Well, go throw some more gasoline on it.

Mommy, Mommy, what happened to all the cat food Tiger wouldn't eat?

Just eat your meatloaf.

Mommy, Mommy, do we have to visit Auntie?

Hush, and keep digging.

Mommy, Mommy, when are we going to have the neighbors for dinner?

You haven't even finished your cousins yet.

Mike: *What's your favorite party game?*

Eddie: *Pin the tail on the donkey.*

Mike: *Oh, that must make your behind really sore.*

Cannibal Mother: *Dear, go get some salt and pepper and some plates.*

Cannibal Son: *But why, Mom?*

Cannibal Mother: *Your sister has just fallen on the barbecue.*

What's cold and green and has a cherry on top?

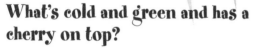

A snot sundae.

Seriously Sick

Everyone knows it's fun to color eggs on Easter. But it's even more fun to make them gross, ugly colors! Instead of dying the eggshells yellow, purple, or green, mix all those colors together to make a yucky brown. Dye your eggs poop-brown or booger-green and then put them in an Easter basket on display.

GROSS-O-METER

In 2002, 38,000 people threw more than 120 tons of tomatoes at each other during the La Tomatilla Festival in Spain. By the end of the festival, streets were running over with tomato juices up to a foot high. Wading home in tomato juice gets a pretty solid seven on the Gross-o-meter scale.

Totally Twisted

Gross out your friends with a box of yuckiness! Get a bunch of grapes and cover them with olive oil. Then put them in a shoebox and cut a hole out of the box just big enough for only your hand. Label the box "Human Eyeballs." Then, with an adult's help, cook some spaghetti, drain it, and add oil. Put that in another box with a hole just big enough for your hand. Label it "Slimy Worms." Invite your friends over and dare them to feel what lurks inside each box.

What's a witch's favorite dessert?

Ice scream.

Customer: Waitress, what's that fly doing on my birthday cake?

Waitress: Laying eggs.

What game do elephants play with mice?

Squash.

How do slugs greet each other on January 1st?

Happy Goo Year!

To find the answer to this knock-knock, cross out all letters that follow these rules:

- Sounds like what you do in the toilet
- Third letter of a common word for "gas"
- First letter of an icky pimple name

When you are finished, read the remaining letters from left to right, and top to bottom.

Knock, knock. Who's there?

PZABPZBEPZRYZPR
APBPBPEYWPHPOP
RABPBERYSTPUZNG
MZEPONMYRBUTPT

Chapter 3

Cannibals, Vampires, and Other Freaky Folks

Did you hear about the cannibal who ate his uncle's wife?

He was an aunt-eater.

Why do cannibals leave space around a body at a funeral?

They need room to serve the appetizers.

What's worse than getting too close to a werewolf?

Getting too close to a werewolf with lice.

How do hairy scary monsters count to 100?

On their warts.

Cannibal 1: *I don't like my wife.*

Cannibal 2: *Perhaps a little pepper would help.*

What does a cannibal call a body on its way to a funeral home?

A moveable feast.

Totally Twisted

Make your own gaping wound with Vaseline, ketchup, cocoa powder, and a paper towel. Mix together a glob of Vaseline and some ketchup. Sprinkle in a bit of cocoa powder. Dip a piece of paper towel in plain Vaseline and stick it on your arm. Mold it so the ends stick up a bit. Then add your wound mixture.

What do you give a dragon with an upset stomach?

Lots of room.

Why did the vampire get fired from his job as zookeeper?

He kept biting the visitors.

How do you help a starving cannibal?

Give him a helping hand.

What does a man-eater call a bunch of bodies in a hearse?

Meals on wheels.

Why did the cannibal get expelled from school?

He kept buttering up the teacher.

What did the cannibal eat while he was on a diet?

Children.

What do vampires do to feel better?

Relax in a blood bath.

What do cannibals call a noontime funeral?

Lunch.

How do vampires travel the ocean?

By blood vessel.

What's a flesh-eater's favorite side dish?

Human beans.

How do you know who the waiter is at a cannibal wedding?

He's the one serving the guests.

GROSS-O-METER

About ten billion minuscule flakes of skin fall off your body every day. If you collected all that skin, by the end of your life you would have eighteen sugar bags full. That's just gross. Dead flaky skin all over the place gets an eight on the Gross-o-meter scale.

Divide the number of spaces between all of your toes by the number of nostrils in your nose.

What number do you get? Collect all the words from the word grid that have this number. Put them in the correct order to find the answer to this riddle:

Why couldn't the caveman hear the pterodactyl go to the bathroom?

4 silent	3 loudly	1 only
1 cavemen	1 poop!	2 Hear
3 too	3 The	4 pterodactyls
4 have	1 Because	3 was
3 wooly	4 "p"!	1 can
1 hear	3 burping	3 mammoth
4 a	2 what?	4 Because

Rain?

Why did Dracula's girlfriend dump him?

The relationship was very draining.

What did the alien say when he met the cat?

Take me to your litter.

What do you get if you cross a snowman and a vampire?

Frostbite.

What do you call a bunch of man-eaters that like sweaty feet?

Odor eaters.

Foul Language

Bromhidrosis

You know how sometimes at the end of a hot day you take off your shoes and socks only to be overwhelmed by an awful smell? It's sometimes enough to clear out a whole room! Well, this condition of stinky feet actually has a very scientific name: bromhidrosis. Some simple powder or foot deodorizer is an easy cure.

What does a cannibal call a man in a hammock?

Breakfast in bed.

Why did the cannibal eat the tightrope walker?

He wanted a balanced meal.

How did the monster stop her son from biting his nails?

She knocked his teeth out.

Why did the cannibal eat the brains of his victims?

It gave him food for thought.

Why couldn't the cannibal kids have their pets at the dinner table?

Pets are only served at breakfast.

What do witches use to style their hair?

Scare spray.

What do cannibals call a burial at sea?

Seafood.

Why did the vampire get taken away in a straitjacket?

He had gone batty.

Why do cannibals eat by candlelight?

So they can see who's being served.

How did the werewolf send his birthday cards?

By hair-mail.

What did the vampire eat after he had his teeth pulled?

The dentist.

What do sea monsters eat for dinner?

Fish and ships.

Did you hear about the young cannibal who hated his teacher?

His mother suggested he try her with ketchup.

What do you call a great big sea monster that hangs people?

The loch noose monster.

Why do people get so upset when a vampire bites them?

It's a drain in the neck.

What do you get if you cross a piranha with your nose?

Use a reverse alphabet code (A=Z, B=Y, C=X, etc.) to figure out the answer to this riddle!

R wlm'g pmld,
yfg R dlfowm'g
dzmg gl krxp rg!

Seriously Sick

Ever wonder which muscle in the human body is the biggest? It's your gluteus maximus, or the muscle in your rear end. This muscle helps to hold you upright and also helps you swing your legs. Without the gluteus maximus, you couldn't sit *or* stand!

Why don't cannibals ever oversleep?

They don't want to be breakfast.

Why didn't the cannibal want to go to the crematorium for lunch?

They overcook everything.

What kind of mail does Dracula receive after doing a movie?

Fang mail.

What happens if you make a cannibal angry?

You end up in hot water.

What did the teacher give the cannibals?

Their first taste of education.

How do you tell when two monsters are getting along?

They see eye to eye to eye.

How did the cannibal like his guests?

Medium well.

What happened to the cannibal who ate the comedian?

He felt a little funny.

GROSS-O-METER

Pierre Beauchemin was the most flexible man in the world. He once dislocated both his legs to prove that he could fit in a box the size of a picnic basket. Doing strange things to your body to fit in unusually small places gets a nine on the Gross-o-meter scale.

How did the monster count to thirty-two?

On his fingers.

What kind of tiles did the witch have installed in her bathroom?

Reptiles.

How do you know if you have a monster in your bathtub?

The shower curtain won't close.

What is a cannibal's favorite dessert?

Ladyfingers.

What do body snatchers call it when they dig up a body and bring it home?

Take out.

Why do witches wear green eye shadow?

They like the way it matches their teeth.

What do vampires eat with their sandwiches?

Pickled organs.

Why did the single cannibal woman visit a matchmaker?

She was looking for an edible bachelor.

Why wouldn't the vampire eat his soup?

It clotted.

What did the cannibal say to his new neighbors?

I would love to have you for dinner sometime.

What's a vampire's favorite drink?

A Bloody Mary.

Why do cannibals feel they are helping the environment?

They control overpopulation.

What do cannibals eat when they go to a restaurant?

The waiter.

What did they say to the cannibal who was late for dinner?

Everybody's already eaten!

Why wasn't there any food left at the monster café?

Because everybody there was a goblin'.

What does a vampire on a diet drink?

Blood light.

The silly reply to this statement is hidden in the letter grid. To find it, color in all the letters *except* P–U. When you're finished, read the dark letters from left to right and top to bottom.

"Your brother sure is spoiled!"

```
N P O P H P E S P N O P
T U P H U P U E A P L W
A U P Y P S P S P M E P
P L U L U P P S P T P H
P U A T P U W P A P Y P
```

Totally Twisted

Make your own gross pie. Get a cooked pie shell, and combine a cup and a half of milk, one cup of flour, two eggs, and a little green food coloring in a bowl. With adult supervision, heat the mixture on low on the stove top. Pour the mixture into the pie crust. Add Gummy worms and let cool. Freeze pie before serving.

What's a cannibal's favorite wine?

One with lots of body.

Why did the vampire get sick after lunch?

He ate a stake sandwich.

Why did the monster eat his watch?

He was trying to kill time.

Did you hear about the vampire who keeps his teeth in the freezer?

He gives his victims frostbite.

Did you hear about the monster that threw up?

It was all over town.

What does a vampire say to his victims?

It's been nice gnawing you.

How do you know when there's a huge monster under the bed?

Your face touches the ceiling.

Why do mother monsters read to their children?

To engross them.

Foul Language

Sputum

This is basically another word for phlegm, or that mucus that seeps into your throat and makes you gag. If you're congested, your respiratory system makes a lot of sputum and you really have no choice but to spit it up or swallow it.

Why do vampires drink blood?
Grape juice makes them burp.

Why did the cannibal join the police department?
So he could grill his suspects.

Why don't cannibals like to eat internal organs?
They are hard to stomach.

What do you get when you cross a vampire with a nun?
A nasty habit.

What's worse than being a 300-pound witch?
Being her broom.

What do you call a vampire child's allowance for lunch?
Blood money.

What do cannibals call body parts that have been removed during surgery?
Leftovers.

What's it called when cannibals use embalming fluid on a body?
Seasoning.

Seriously Sick
Believe it or not, there are thousands of spores in the air just waiting to assault you. They're all over you, in every part of your room, and even on the food you eat. When they find a good landing place—usually some old leftover food or a dead animal—they implant themselves, causing gross, fuzzy mold.

Why don't cannibals eat clowns?
Because they taste funny.

What's yellow and smells of dead humans?
Cannibal puke.

Why did the vampire go to art school?
He needed to draw blood.

What happened when the gross green monster appeared on stage?

He got a lot of ooze and ahs.

What game do cannibals love to play?

Swallow the leader.

Why was the Cyclops such an attentive teacher?

He only had one pupil.

Why do cannibals like having their relatives for dinner?

It gives them a chance to serve loved ones.

Why don't vampires like steak?

It goes right through them.

Why don't man-eaters eat bratty, rich kids?

Because they're spoiled.

Chapter 4
Atrocious Animals

What did the leopard say after eating the tourist?

That hit the spot.

Why do gorillas have such big nostrils?

Because they have big fingers.

Fred: My canary died of the flu.

Ed: How did that happen?

Fred: He flew into a car.

What do you call it when one vulture throws a dead animal at another vulture?

A food fight.

What do you call a man who's been mauled by a tiger?

Gord.

Customer: I'd like to buy a bird, please.

Clerk: I've got the perfect one. She sings and she's got red feathers.

Customer: Never mind that, how long does she take to cook?

What did Jimmy say when his mother asked if he put the cat out?

Is the cat on fire again?

I am such a slimy creature that I can turn a jar of water into a big slimy mess in a matter of seconds. Not only that, I eat my prey from the inside out, leaving nothing but a bag of skin and bones. **What am I?**

A hagfish.

What's wet, stinks, and goes thump de thump de thump?

A skunk in the dryer.

What's gray and furry on the inside and white on the outside?

A mouse sandwich.

What do you call a brontosaurus trapped in a glacier?

A fossicle.

Why did the mother hen roll her eggs around the henhouse?

She liked playing with children.

What do you do if you find a boa constrictor in your toilet?

Wait until he's finished.

How did the farmer feel when a bird pooped in his eye?

He was thankful that pigs can't fly.

Son: *The dog just ate the dinner mom made for us.*

Father: *Don't worry, son, we'll get you a new dog.*

How do you make your puppy disappear?

Use Spot remover.

Mother: *Why did you pull the dog's tail?*

Son: *I didn't pull it. I was standing on it and he pulled it.*

What am I?

I only have hair in one place on my body and it's not on my head. It's inside my mouth! When I'm born, my skin is so transparent you can see my insides. I live with others like me in deep, dark underground tunnels. I may be ugly, but I'm not alone.

What am I?

A naked mole rat.

Snot Milk?

This kid just heard a very funny joke. He laughed so hard that the chocolate milk he was drinking came out his nose! See if you can find the shadow that matches the drawing of this gross-out gaffaw.

What is small, furry, and smells like bacon?

A hamster.

Why aren't elephants allowed in public swimming pools?

They always drop their trunks.

What's the difference between a werewolf and a mean rabbit?

One is a hairy beast and the other is a beastly hare.

What do you call a frog with no back legs?

Unhoppy.

What did the rooster say when he stepped in cow poop?

Cock-a-doodle-poo.

What do you call your cat when he gets stuck in the dryer?

Fluffy.

What's black and white and red all over?

A zebra being eaten by a lion.

What happened to the cat that crashed into the screen door?

He strained himself.

What has twelve legs, six ears, a foul odor, and one eye?

Three blind mice and half a rotten fish.

What do you get when you cross a band with a chimpanzee?

A chimp-phony.

What am I?

If you try to catch me I will turn into a slippery glob of mucus and you'll never be able to hold me in your grip. I do this as a defense mechanism so no one can turn me into their dinner. I live underwater.
What am I?

An eel.

Why did the elephant paint himself brown?

So he could hide in a pile of manure.

Why was the kangaroo so upset after she'd been pick-pocketed?

Her whole family was missing.

Why are all the dogs raving about the newest dog food?

It tastes like the mailman.

What do you call a cat with a wooden leg?

Peg.

What's the difference between a rat and your spaghetti?

The rat won't slip off the fork when you go to eat it.

What's black and white and black and white?

A penguin rolling down a mountain.

What did one frog say to the other?

Time's sure fun when you're having flies.

Farmer: I had to shoot the cow.
Farmer's wife: Was she mad?
Farmer: She wasn't too happy about it.

Mother: Why did you put a toad in your brother's bed?
Sister: I couldn't find a python.

What do you call a dancing pig?

Shakin' bacon.

Delivery Man: Your dog bit my leg.
Lady: Did you put anything on it?
Delivery Man: No, he seemed to like it just the way it was.

When is a sheep like a dog?

When it has fleece.

GROSS-O-METER

Owls trap their prey and then swallow it whole. That means fur, skin, bones—everything. Then, as if that weren't gross enough, they cough up the fur, skin, and bones in a giant ball of grossness. They keep the meat down and digest it. Regurgitating a mouse gets an eight on the Gross-o-meter scale.

What do you get if you cross a sheep with a black belt in karate?

Lamb chops.

What did the cat call the mouse?

Breakfast.

Why can't skunks keep secrets?

Someone is always catching wind of them.

Why do mother birds puke in their babies' mouths?

They want to send them out with a hot breakfast.

Sam: *Our new dog is like a member of the family.*

John: *I can see the resemblance.*

What am I?

Am I dead or alive? You'll never know. If you get too near, I may simply pretend to die. I may turn upside down, throw back my head, and even hold my mouth open. If I'm faking, you don't want to come too close. This is when I'll attack. **What am I?**

A hognose snake.

GROSS-O-METER

In 1945, Lloyd Olsen of Colorado cut the head off a chicken. The chicken, named Mike, lived for eighteen months without a head. The chicken became a celebrity and even went on tour. Headless chickens running around the yard rate a ten on the Gross-o-meter scale.

What was the pig's favorite karate move?

The pork chop.

Why did the vulture cross the road?

He had fowl reasons.

What happened to the boy who sat under the cow?

He got a pat on the head.

What did one toad say to the other?

Warts new?

What do you have left if a pig eats all your watermelon?

Pork rinds.

What do lions call antelopes?

Fast food.

Why did the lion feel sick after every meal?

It's hard to keep a good man down.

Foul Language

Scat

Have you ever been walking through a wooded area and all of a sudden you feel something mushy under your shoe? Chances are, you stepped in scat. Scat is the little poop pellets left behind by deer, rabbits, or other wildlife.

Why didn't the mother pig let her piglets play with toads?

She didn't want them to turn into wart hogs.

What happened to the hen that ate gun powder?

She laid hen grenades.

What did the pig play at the casino?

The slop machines.

Why was the mouse crying?

He found out his father was a rat.

What kind of shark would never eat a woman?

A man-eating shark.

What happens if you kiss an electric eel?

You have a shocking experience.

What's grosser than a three-headed spider with forty eyes?

Not much.

Why is a toothless dog like a tree?

It has more bark than bite.

Sick Change

You can change a normal word into a gross-out word by simply changing a letter!
Try it and pee—oops, that should be try it and <u>see</u>!

Change a small wagon
to smelly gas

to _____

Change a flat piece of wood
to a crusty wound cover

to _____

Change a tangle of string
to a booger

to _____

Change the center of a
peach to a pimple

to _____

Change a swollen spot
to a belch

to _____

Change a large ring made
of metal to a pile of #2

to _____

Why did Johnny put a dead mouse on the end of his fish hook?

He was fishing for catfish.

What do you call a woodpecker without a beak?

A head-banger.

Why did the bald man walk around with a rabbit on his head?

He really wanted some hare.

Seriously Sick

Did you know that bats eat about 100 bugs per second? Well, that's not even the gross part. In some parts of the world, bats are more than just bug-catchers. Broiled or boiled, fried or barbecued, these creatures make great meals. Dipping sauce, anyone?

How do you know owls are smarter than chickens?

You've never eaten fried owl, have you?

Why was the fish offended?

Because the sea weed.

Why are cats luckier than frogs?

Frogs croak all the time, and cats only croak nine times.

What do you get when you cross a young goat with a pig?

A dirty kid.

What's the worst thing that can happen to a bat while it's sleeping?

Diarrhea.

What's a frog's favorite flower?

The crocus.

What says "Gobble, gobble . . . catch me if you can"?

A suicidal turkey.

What do you get if you cross a slug with a cocker spaniel?

A dog that slithers on the ground after it rains.

What did the cat do after he ate the cheese?

Waited for the mouse with baited breath.

What do you get when you cross a dog with a solider?

A pooping trooper.

Fred: It's the dog days of summer.
Ed: How do you know?
Fred: I just stepped in a poodle.

What's worse than seeing a shark's fins in the water?

Seeing its teeth.

What am I?

I look like a giant grub slithering around on the ocean floor. Some say I am a cross between a fish and a reptile. My species has been around a long time. You will very rarely see me, so consider yourself lucky if you get a glimpse. **What am I?**

An axolotl.

Totally Twisted

Make some fake snot sculptures for your art collection. You'll need two tablespoons of glue, a quarter cup of water, a few drops of green food coloring, and yellow raisins. Stir it all together in a paper cup or plastic bowl and then let dry. Finally, fake a sneeze into the cup.

What has four legs and flies?
A dead cow.

How did the depressed frog die?
He kermitted suicide.

What did the angry pig say to his wife?
You take me for grunted.

What sound does a dog make when it's throwing up?
Barf, barf.

What am I?

I can be very deceiving to my enemies. I live in the deep, dark jungle and I look like a vine twisted around a tree. When no one is looking, I slither along. If you're a small animal and you come too near, I'll make dinner out of you!
What am I?

A vine snake.

How do you get a whole set of teeth for free?
Make a lion angry.

On what day of the week do lions eat people?
Chewsday.

How do you turn a snake into a vegetable?
Slam it against a rock and you have squash.

Knock Knock
Who's there?
Howard.
Howard who?
Howard I know the dog would puke if I fed him cat poop?

What's black and white and flat?
A penguin that's been run over by a steam roller.

What's red and green and spins around really fast?
A frog in a blender.

What happened to the man who tried to cross a lion with a goat?
He had to get a new goat.

Did you hear about the dog that got first prize at the cat show?

He ate the first prize cat.

You know what they say about a bird in hand?

It poops on your wrist.

Why did the musical band eat the rabbit?

They wanted to play hip hop.

What animal always pukes after it eats?

The yak.

What's green and hangs from trees?

Monkey snot.

How do you know when you're eating rabbit pie?

It has hares in it.

Where do bats stay while they're on vacation?

The Caved Inn.

What do you get if you pour boiling water down a rabbit hole?

A hot, cross bunny.

Why did Jim put his German shepherd in the oven?

He wanted a hot dog.

What's worse than five dead cats in one garbage can?

One dead cat in five garbage cans.

Where do pigs go when they are sick?
The hog-spital.

Why did the frog ride a motorcycle with his mouth open?

He thought it would be easier to catch flies.

What did the pig do when he identified the butcher in a police lineup?

He squealed.

What do you get when you feed a cow too many worms?

Disgusting milk.

What kind of fish don't swim?

Dead ones.

What does a shark call a family he sees on the beach?

A five-course meal.

What do you get when you cross an ape with a bunch of earthworms?

Giant holes in the garden.

When is fishing bad for you?

When you're a worm.

What do you call a fairy that never showers?

To find out the answer to this riddle, figure out which letters are described by each fraction. Print the letters, in order, in the boxes from left to right.

1. First 2/5 of STALE
2. First 1/3 of INFECT
3. Last 1/2 of PUKE
4. Middle 1/3 of MORBID
5. Last 3/5 of SMELL

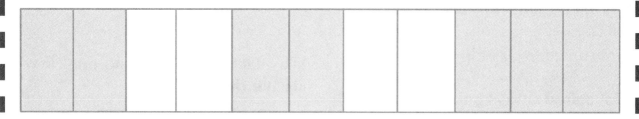

Ed: *We just sold our sheep for $100.00.*
Fred: *We just sold our new puppy.*
Ed: *What did you sell it for?*
Fred: *For pooping on the floor.*

What does a chicken that lays a square egg say?

Ouch.

What do you get if you cross an elephant with a cockroach?

I don't know, but if it crawls up your wall, you'd better get a new house.

What happened to the bear that ate a clock?

He got ticks.

What do you give a pig with pimples?

Oinkment.

Foul Language

Venom
Many creepy creatures, such as snakes and scorpions, have a very deadly way of defending themselves. Some of them can spew out enough venom, or poison, through their fangs, claws, or stingers to paralyze or even kill prey.

What do you get if you cross a skunk with a porcupine?

A stinky pin cushion.

What kind of bird do cats eat?

Swallows.

What did the man say when his dog got hit by a train?

Doggone.

What would we need if pigs really could fly?

Bigger umbrellas.

Little Mona: *I'd like to buy a kitty cat. How much do they cost?*

Shop Owner: *Fifty dollars apiece.*

Little Mona: *Oh no, how much is a whole one?*

What is green and prickly?

A sick porcupine.

Why do some animals eat their young?

They love them to death.

What do you call it when a chicken stumbles in the road?

A road trip.

What do you call a fish with no eyes?

Fsh.

Why are goldfish orange?

The water makes them rusty.

What happens when you put a baby goat in a blender?

You get a crazy mixed-up kid.

Why did the duck cross the road during rush hour?

To show the chicken he had guts.

Foul Language

Rabies

Rabies is one scary virus. Humans can only get this virus if an infected animal bites them. Rabid animals may foam at the mouth, act strangely, and tend to look sick. Rabies is common in raccoons, wolves, and other wild animals that might live near your home—so be careful!

What smells of fish parts and goes round and round?

A goldfish in a washing machine during spin cycle.

What do you get if you cross a goat with a baby cow?

Half and calf.

How do you know a sick frog when you see one?

He croaks out of both ends.

How does a cow get even when someone makes her mad?

She creams him.

Atrocious Animals

Where do you find a no-legged cat?
Right where you left him.

Why was the chicken kicked out of school?
He was being fowl.

What happened to the wolf that swallowed a sheep?
He felt baaaaaaaaad.

What do you call a deer with no eyes?
No eye deer.

What sound does a cat make before it eats a mouse?
The hiss of death.

What did the mother lion say to her cub who was chasing a man around a tree?
Stop playing with your food.

What did the piranha say when the students took a class trip to the beach?
Fresh meat just arrived!

Who goes into a tiger's den and comes out in one piece?
The tiger.

What did the freshly bathed dog say to the insect?
Long time no flea.

What's black and white and red all over?
A skunk with poison ivy.

What does a pig call his hot date?
Fine swine.

Did you hear about the limping dog?
He laid down to chew a bone and when he got up he only had three legs.

What do you get if you cross an eel and a sponge?
A shock absorber.

What do you get when you put a parrot in a blender?
Shredded tweet.

What's a vulture's favorite snack?
Road pie.

How do you raise a kitten?
By its neck.

What do you find under the feet of an elephant?

Squished mice.

Why did the turkey stop eating his dinner?

He was already stuffed.

How do you keep a rooster from waking you up in the morning?

Cook him the night before.

Why do giraffes have such long necks?

Because their feet stink.

What did the lady say when her parrot died?

Polygon.

Why did the girl laugh when the cow fell off the cliff?

There's no point in crying over spilled milk.

What words do skunks live by?

Eat, stink, and be merry.

Why did the dog laugh after chewing the bone?

It was a funny bone.

What did the snake say to his young son?

Stop your crying and viper your nose.

What's the definition of a slick chick?

Poultry that slid into a puddle of motor oil.

What does an aardvark take for indigestion?

Anta-seltzer.

What do you call a cow with no legs?

Ground beef.

What do frogs love to drink more than anything else?

Croaka-Cola.

What do you call a sheep in a rainstorm?

A wet blanket.

What do you get when you put a leopard in your dishwasher?

Spotty dishes.

What is black and white and red all over?

A sunburned penguin.

Chapter 5

Horrible Humans

Why did Mary hold up an ax to her sibling?

She always wanted a half sister.

What's the difference between Gross Grandma's cooking and a pile of slugs?

Gross Grandma's cooking comes on a plate.

Why are executioners so smart?

Because they always watch the noose.

Knock Knock

Who's there?
Huron.
Huron who?
Huron my toe! Ouch!

Bar of soap: *"Sometimes I think I have the worst job in the world."*

Toilet paper: *"Think again."*

Did you hear about the restaurant where you could eat dirt cheap?

Who wants to eat dirt?

What did one booger say to the other?

You think you're funny, but you're snot.

Why did Ned's mom say he ate like a bird?

He kept eating worms.

What happened to the mad scientist who fell into the bubbling acid?

He became absorbed in his work.

Knock Knock

Who's there?
One shoe.
One shoe who?
One shoe bathe once in a while?

What do you call a knight who picks his nose?

Sir Picks-a-lot.

Why did Jimmy tell his sister she reminded him of the sea?

Because he made her sick.

Seriously Sick

Did you ever hear the saying "Don't throw the baby out with the bath water"? Long ago only one bathtub full of water was used to bathe an entire family. The oldest went first, so by the time the baby was bathed, the water was so dirty you could hardly see him.

How do you make a handkerchief dance?

Put a little boogie in it.

Why did the leper go back into the shower?

He forgot his head and shoulders.

Why did the sword swallower switch to pins and needles?

He needed to lose weight.

What is it called when someone gets hit in the face with slime?

Goo-lash.

What do you call a man with no arms or legs holding up your car?

Jack.

Why did everyone tell the old hag she looked like a million bucks?

Because she was green and wrinkled.

Why do stabbing victims hate the ocean?

They don't like to pour salt in their wounds.

Foul Language

Plaque

This is a clear, sticky substance that builds up on your teeth. It is made up of leftover food and mucus. If you don't brush regularly, it will spread to your gums and tongue. It can cause cavities, gum disease, and really bad breath. Ew!

What do you call a man who sticks his right hand in an alligator's mouth?

Lefty.

What do babies with dirty diapers and security officers have in common?

They are both on duty.

What did the magician say to the fisherman?

Pick a cod, any cod.

Seriously Sick

Have you ever wondered what people did before indoor plumbing? If you lived in a crowded city, you peed and pooped in buckets kept in your bedroom. When the buckets were filled, you'd simply throw the nasty mix right out your windows and into the street! Now, there's a good use for an umbrella.

Knock Knock

Who's there?
Urine.
Urine who?
Urine my way!

What happened when Jimmy's mother said she was going to take him to the zoo?

His father said not to bother—if the zoo wanted Jimmy, they could come and get him.

What did one toilet say to the other?

You look a little flushed.

Why did the drummer bring the chicken to band practice?

He needed new drumsticks.

Little Johnny: Mother, do you have holes in your underwear?

Mother: No, of course not.
Little Johnny: Well, then how do you get your feet through?

How do you get to the hospital in a hurry?

Stand in front of a bus.

Horrible Humans

What did the audience do when the comedian bent over too far?

Cracked up.

When a knight dies in battle, what do they put on his gravestone?

Rust in peace.

What has a broom and flies?

A janitor covered in poop.

How come Johnny's mother used to say he was going to drive her to her grave?

Well, you don't expect her to walk, do you?

Seriously Sick

Earwax in your ear canal helps block out all the nasty stuff trying to get in there. You know, like dirt, dust, small insects, even germs. You've got over 2,000 glands in your ear working hard to make this wax.

How do you know if someone has a fake eye?

It usually comes out in conversation.

What happens to writers who don't make it to heaven?

They become ghost writers.

How did the man in the electric chair pay for his last meal?

He charged it.

Why do doctors study a lot before prescribing medicine for bad skin diseases?

They don't want to be rash.

Sluuuurp

These two sloppy slurpers are both eating bowls of soup. Can you find the 10 differences between the two?

Strange Soup

Some people make soup out of some pretty weird ingredients! Unscramble the letters at the bottom of this page to find the names of four different and unusual soups. Would you eat these?

IPCSORON UPOS

DIBR TENS UOSP

KHSAR INF POUS

XOLATI OSUP

GROSS-O-METER

A man in India named Radhakant Bajpai gets the award for the longest ear hair in the world, at over five inches long. Now, imagine that ear hair falling into your peanut butter sandwich. That gets a solid ten on the Gross-o-meter scale.

Pete: My doctor said to drink some tea after a hot bath.

Bob: Did you drink the tea?

Pete: Well, I haven't finished drinking the hot bath yet.

How did Sally Picker hurt her finger?

The school bully broke her nose.

Did you hear about the constipated musician?

He couldn't finish his last movement.

What are the two things that stopped Sheila from becoming a ballerina?

Her feet.

How do you make a baby drink?

Stick it in a blender.

Did you hear about the woman who thought she had the face of a sixteen year old?

Her husband told her to give it back.

What did the poor person do when he couldn't afford shoes?

He painted his feet and tied his toes together.

Why did the little boy bury his parents?

He wanted to grow a family tree.

What do you call the first person to ever discover fire?

Crispy.

What did Sven say when his brother Hans fell off the cliff?

Look Mom, no Hans.

What happened when the girl found out her future husband had a wooden leg?

She broke it off.

What usually runs in big families?

Noses.

Foul Language

Halitosis

This is a fancy word for stinky breath. If you eat lots of garlic or other strong-smelling foods and you start to notice people backing away from you, chances are you're suffering from a bad case of halitosis. Try brushing your teeth more often and carrying some breath mints in your pocket from now on.

Did you hear about the kid who missed his mother?

His father told him to take another shot.

What's worse than a plain old fart?

A fart with a lump in it.

What do you call a restaurant where everyone picks their nose?

Booger King.

GROSS-O-METER

Long before doctors knew about germs, they would do surgery without washing their hands first. Hospitals were deadly places. Having a doctor stick his dirty fingers into a gaping wound while spreading thousands of germs rates a nine on the Gross-o-meter scale.

Knock Knock

Who's there?
Stella.
Stella who?
Stella 'fraid you'll poop in your pants?

What did one virus say to another?

Stay away, I think I've got penicillin.

What time is it when you sit on a sharp object?

Springtime.

Why was the cross-eyed teacher so upset?

He couldn't control his pupils.

What's the best way to talk to someone with bad breath?

From far away.

What do you do when your nose goes on strike?

Picket.

What do you call a person who makes two trips to Europe and doesn't bathe?

A dirty double-crosser.

What's the hardest part about sky diving?

The ground.

What did the caveman say when he saw bugs crawling on his dinner?

Mmmm . . . appetizers!

Where's the proper place to save rotten toenails?

In a nail file.

What's the difference between a window shop and a poke in the eyes in Italy?

One makes Venetian blinds and the other makes Venetians blind.

On what day of the week do lions eat people?

To find the answer to this gross riddle, fill in the words that answer each description below. Then read down the shaded column. We left you some S-C-R-A-P-S to get you started!

1. To chew with a crackling sound
2. To chew noisily
3. Flesh of an animal used as food
4. Take little bites again and again
5. To eat richly on a special occasion
6. One who is eating
7. What you do after you chew
8. Not neat; messy

What do you call a person with three ears, four eyes, and warts all over his face?

Ugly.

Did you hear about the patient who complained that he needed something for his liver?

The doctor told him to try adding onions.

What did Sally see when her friend Dawn bent over?

The crack of dawn.

What did the lady say to the man who came to the door with a funny face?

Thanks, but I've already got one.

Fred: Whenever I take my girlfriend out for dinner she eats her head off.

Ed: Stop complaining. She looks better that way.

Knock Knock
Who's there?
Blue.
Blue who?
Blue your nose on your sleeve again?

Horrible Humans

Why was the sword swallower arrested?

He coughed and killed two people.

How come the millionaire never showered?

He was filthy rich.

Why don't burn victims like to eat in the hospital?

The food makes their skin crawl.

Why did the toilet paper run down the mountain?

It wanted to get to the bottom.

What did one eye say to the other?

Between you and me, I think something smells.

What do you get when you mix tacos and a person who's not feeling so good?

I don't know, but you're standing in it.

What's it called when you pick your nose and hide it for later?

The pick and save.

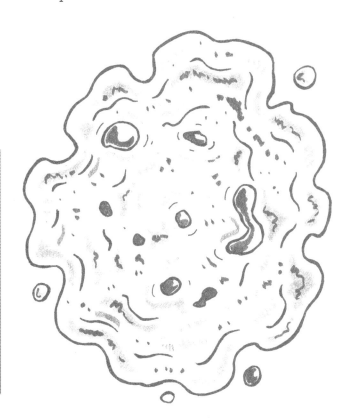

GROSS-O-METER

In the not-too-distant past, doctors would actually taste a patient's pee to see if it was sweet. If it was too sweet, that meant the patient might have a disease called diabetes. Pee-drinking ranks a solid ten on the Gross-o-meter scale. Would you like a cookie with that?

What do you call a person with no arms or legs floating in the water?

Bob.

What was the farmer able to prove when the chicken got run over by a steamroller?

That it had a lot of guts.

Did you ever see the movie "Constipation"?

It never came out.

What am I?

I am a disease that infects your nose. You'll feel mucus building up and getting really goopy as I make it a breeding ground for bacteria. Soon the mucus will start to rot and turn into green or black crust. Your nose will begin to stink.
What am I?

Rhinitis.

Why did the kids call Johnny "flat-face"?

Because he kept his nose to the grindstone.

What's worse than two Siamese twins connected at the mouth?

Watching one of them throw up.

What do you get if you slime a telephone worker?

A smooth operator.

Why did the baby cross the road?

He was stapled to the chicken.

How do you stop a sleepwalker?

Cover the floor with tacks.

What's worse than a boy who picks his nose?

A boy who picks someone else's nose.

Do you know about Larry the Loafer?

He's so lazy that he sticks his nose out the window so the wind will blow it for him.

What happens when you cross a judge with poison ivy?

You get rash decisions.

How do you catch dandruff?

Shake your head over a paper bag.

What happened to the thief who stole from the blood bank?

He was caught red-handed.

Where do butchers go to dance?

The Meat Ball.

Knock Knock

Who's there?

Wendy.

Wendy who?

Wendy sneezes come,

snot goes everywhere.

Foul Language

Bile

This is yellow or greenish liquid that comes from your liver. Its job is to break down fats in your body. When it's done doing its job, it becomes part of your poop. As a matter of fact, that's what gives your poop its nice color.

Why was the fireman so upset?

He ran into an old flame.

Patient: Doctor, I threw my back out, what should I do?

Doctor: Maybe you can catch the garbage truck before it leaves.

What happened to the man who put his false teeth in backwards?

He ate himself.

How did the garbage man break up with his girlfriend?

He dumped her.

What kind of skin problem does a beekeeper have?

Hives.

What's the best cure for a headache?

Put your head through the window and the pane will go away.

What do people with weak bladders and people who wear old stockings have in common?

They both get runs down their legs.

Customer: The water in this glass is cloudy.
Waiter: Don't worry—the water's fine.
It's just the glass that's cloudy.

Why didn't the photographer develop his pictures of the boogeyman?

He was afraid to be alone in the dark with them.

Knock Knock

Who's there?
Emma.
Emma who?
Emma 'fraid you have an ugly face.

What do you call a vegetarian with diarrhea?

A salad shooter.

What did the first mate see in the toilet?

The captain's log.

What did the drooling butler say to the guests when he answered the door?

Greetings and salivations.

If vegetarians only eat vegetables, what do you call humans that eat other humans?

Sick.

What am I?

I can be found inside your mouth. I'm a slippery mix of mucus, protein, salt, and water. I help you chew and digest your food. Sometimes when you sleep I trickle out the side of your mouth. **What am I?**

Saliva.

Did you hear what happened to the man who lost his left arm and leg in an accident?

He's all right now.

What kind of underwear is good for putting out fires?

Pantyhose.

What does a liar do when he's sleeping?

He lies still.

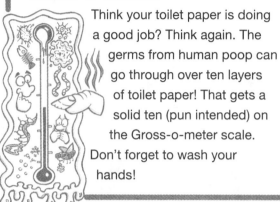

GROSS-O-METER

Think your toilet paper is doing a good job? Think again. The germs from human poop can go through over ten layers of toilet paper! That gets a solid ten (pun intended) on the Gross-o-meter scale. Don't forget to wash your hands!

Why did they lock up the man who thought he was a bird?

He was a raven lunatic.

What's the difference between a thermometer that goes in your bottom and one that goes in your mouth?

The taste.

Why was everyone amazed when they saw the Catskill Mountains?

Because cats usually only kill mice.

Mother: Why do you play the same song on the piano over and over?
Son: I find it haunting.
Mother: It should haunt you—you murdered it!

What happened to the thief who fell into the wet cement?

He went on to become a hardened criminal.

Patient: Is there anything else I can do for my pimples?
Doctor: No, that's zit.

Knock Knock

Who's there?

Goose.

Goose who?

Goose see a doctor, you look horrible.

What kind of training do you need to be a garbage collector?

None, you pick it up as you go along.

B-ughs!

Answer these questions about Bart's bug collection:

Are there more spiders or roaches?

If each fly has 6 legs, how many fly legs are there?

Which mosquito has just bitten someone? How can you tell?

SPIDER

ROACH

FLY

MOSQUITO

Why did the office aide chop off her fingers?

So she could write shorthand.

Why don't lepers like comedy shows?

It makes them laugh their heads off.

Did you hear about the constipated banker?

He couldn't budget.

Why was the teacher so upset when her eye fell out of her head?

She couldn't bear to lose another pupil.

Fred: *My brother does great farmyard impressions.*

Ted: *What animal does he sound like?*
Fred: *He doesn't, he just smells like a pig.*

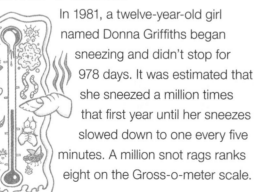

GROSS-O-METER

In 1981, a twelve-year-old girl named Donna Griffiths began sneezing and didn't stop for 978 days. It was estimated that she sneezed a million times that first year until her sneezes slowed down to one every five minutes. A million snot rags ranks eight on the Gross-o-meter scale.

What do you call a person lying in front of your door?

Matt.

Fred: *This morning I gave my brother soap flakes for breakfast instead of corn flakes.*
Ed: *What happened?*
Fred: *He was so mad, he started foaming at the mouth.*

What do you call a leper who has good luck?

A leper-chaun.

What do you call it when a boy vomits up his steak?

Up-chuck.

How did the woman feel after she got run over by a car?

Tired.

How did the dunce burn his ear?

He got a telephone call while he was ironing.

There are three men in the bathroom. One is rushing toward the stall, one is on his way out, and the other is inside the stall. What nationalities are they?

Russian, Finnish, and European.

What's the medical term for a lady who throws up all the time?

Girl hurl.

How many people does it take to wallpaper a room?

Two, but only if they are thinly sliced.

Did you hear about the girl who had long blonde hair growing down her back?

Pity it didn't grow on her head.

How did the leper get into a car accident?

He left his foot on the gas pedal.

What am I?

I am a fungus that thrives in warm sweaty areas. My specialty is causing painful cracks and blisters between your toes. I lurk on all types of floors and in your shoes. If I want to be really nasty I'll make one of your toenails my home.
What am I?

Athlete's foot.

What did Jane's mother say when Jane wanted to lick the bowl?

You must flush it like everybody else.

What happened to the man who flushed himself down the toilet?

He committed sewer-cide.

What's the meaning of bravery?

A person with diarrhea chancing a fart.

Patient: My kidneys have been giving me a hard time.

Doctor: Well, just take them back to the butcher.

What do a Slinky and a school bully have in common?

They're both fun to watch tumble down the stairs.

What happened to the man with amnesia when he farted?

It all came back to him.

How did Stinky Joe's mom stop him from biting his nails?

She made him wear shoes.

How do you make anti-freeze?

Hide her sweater.

The Proper Way to Pick

Deep Sea Picking

This is when you pick your nose so deep it's as if you were diving for buried treasure.

Fork Pick

This is when your fingers just aren't long enough to get what's up there, so you use a fork or other tool. This one is not recommended.

Lottery Pick

This is when you've been picking for days on end and finally hit the jackpot. Your excitement is so overwhelming, it's like you've just won a million bucks.

Sad Pickings

This is when you pick your nose just because you are unhappy and it gives you something to do besides think about what's making you sad.

Pick All Day

This is when you are absolutely obsessed with picking your nose. You use more than one finger and you just can't stop picking.

Secret Pick

This is when no one is around and you pick your nose with freedom and joy. You get way up in there, and you even fling what you find all over the room.

Picking with Pride

This is when you're in public, but you just can't resist the urge to pick. So you pick proudly (and hope that no one notices).

The Fake-Out Pick

This is when you pretend you have an itch, but what you're really doing is looking for boogers that may have strayed out of your nostrils.

Surprise Picks

This is when you sneeze and all of a sudden snot comes flying out of your nose and you have to clean it off your friend's shirt. You didn't even need to pick to loosen those boogers.

Flicking Your Pickings

This is when you use your boogers to taunt family members. You leave it on the tip of your finger and threaten to fling it if anyone comes too close.

Why was the boy's mother horrified when he came home with a broken nose?

He couldn't remember who it belonged to.

What did the doctor tell the patient with chronic diarrhea?

It runs in your family.

How do you say constipation in German?

Farfrompoopin.

What happened to the boy who ate a thermometer?

He was dying by degrees.

Why was the student so upset when she learned about the Dead Sea?

She didn't even know it was sick.

What do you call a coward in the electric chair?

Extra crispy chicken.

What's the best way to cure acid indigestion?

Stop drinking acid.

What do you do when someone rolls their eyes at you?

You pick them up and give them back.

Seriously Sick

The average person can pee anywhere from 1.5 to 3.5 pints a day. But did you know that sweat and urine are virtually the same thing? They both contain something called urea, which causes them to smell bad. Pretty gross, huh?

What do you call a bearded woman who grants wishes?

A hairy godmother.

Lady: Am I too late for the garbage truck?
Garbage Truck Driver: Nope, jump right in.

How do you turn an ordinary scientist into a mad scientist?

Punch him in the nose.

What kind of illness do roofers get?

Shingles.

Why should you never pee in a public pool?

The public doesn't swim in your toilet so you shouldn't pee in their pool.

What magic word do you have to say if you want to get rid of your scabs?

Scabracadabra.

What happened to the hunter who was following tracks in the woods?

He got hit by a train.

What happened to the man who cut off his right butt cheek?

He was left behind.

Did you hear about the math teacher who was constipated?

He worked it out with a pencil.

What happened when the customer complained that his meal wasn't fit for a pig?

The waiter said he'd take it back and bring him a meal that *was* fit for a pig.

Why did Silly Sam get a pain in his nose every time he drank a cup of coffee?

He forgot to take the spoon out of the cup before sipping.

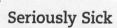

Seriously Sick

Did you ever stick your nose in the bud of a rafflesia flower? This flower smells disgusting, like rotting flesh or spoiled milk. The rafflesia is such a stinker it's even nicknamed the "corpse flower." It's better to give these flowers to your enemies instead of your loved ones.

What did the nice hangman say to his victim?

Is the noose too tight?

Why were the barber's hands so dirty?

No one had been in for a shampoo all day.

What did the waiter say when the customer asked if the chef had pig's feet?

I don't know, he's got his shoes on.

Should kids with the flu go to school?

It's snot for you to decide.

Knock Knock
Who's there?
Warren.
Warren who?
Warren earth did you get such
an ugly face?

How did the school teacher keep the boys on their toes?

He raised the urinals a couple of inches.

Did you hear about the Indian chief who drank twenty cups of tea and went to bed?

He drowned in his tea-pee.

Seriously Sick

Does it ever sound like a bulldozer is whipping through your stomach? Well, that sound comes from the digestive juices sloshing around in there. Your body makes about two gallons of that stuff a day, and it can stay there for up to four hours after you eat.

What do you call a man with mucus in his throat?

Fleming.

How do you keep from dying?

Just stay in the living room.

Knock Knock
Who's there?
Stan.
Stan who?
Stan back, I'm about to vomit.

Did you hear what happened to the plastic surgeon?

He sat in front of a fire and melted.

Why did everyone call Dirty Darrel a wonder child?

Because they all wondered when he was going to take a bath.

What's risky?

Eating raisin bran when your brother can't find his roach collection.

Why should you listen to your father when he tells you not to pick your nose?

Father nose best.

Chapter 6

Beyond the Grave: Ghosts, Ghouls, and Zombies

How does a mummy begin all his letters?

Tomb it may concern.

Why did the goblins show up at the cemetery before dark?

They didn't want to miss the early bird special.

Why didn't anyone want to go to the zombie hair salon?

Because the hairdressers all dyed on the job.

What do you call a dead chicken that haunts you at night?

A poultry-geist.

Did you hear about the ghoul who was sick to his stomach?

It must have been someone he ate.

What do ghouls eat for dinner?

A three-corpse meal.

Where do ghouls go on vacation?

Lake Eerie.

What did the zombie's friend say to him when he introduced his girlfriend?

Oh my, where did you dig her up?

Why do demons and ghouls go together so well?

Because demons are a ghoul's best friend.

GROSS-O-METER

In some ancient societies people honored their dead by eating them. Most of the body was cooked, except the brain. The brain was eaten raw. Eating the raw brain of your dear Uncle Harry gets a ten on the Gross-o-meter scale.

GROSS-O-METER

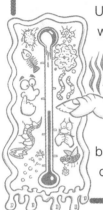

Until about sixty years ago, coffins were very rarely made to fit each person's body size. If you happened to be extra tall, you were out of luck. Undertakers would break a dead person's ankles and fold them over backward to fit. That ranks a nine on the Gross-o-meter scale.

What did one sick casket say to the other?

Is that you coffin?

How does a person who cremates bodies make his money?

He urns it.

Why was the mortuary makeup artist fired?

Everyone thought she was a stiff.

When is it not a good time to bury someone?

When he is still breathing.

Knock Knock

Who's there?
Turner.
Turner who?
Turner 'round—there's a giant ghoul right behind you!

Why did the zombie study Latin?

He wanted to learn a dead language.

What was the gravedigger's favorite song?

Oh What a Beautiful Mourning.

Seriously Sick

In the past, people were sometimes accidentally buried before they were actually dead! This became such a common occurrence that something had to be done. Mourners began tying strings attached to bells around the fingers of the dead before the burial. This way, if someone was really still alive, he simply had to ring the bell for help.

What About Jimmy?

There are three different letters missing from this riddle.
Once you fill in the blanks, you will find out
what happened to Jimmy!

Wh_t h_pp_n_d wh_n
Jimmy's m_th_r s_id
sh_ w_s g_ing t_ t_k_
Jimmy t_ th_ z___?

Jimmy's br_th_r s_id
"D_n't b_th_r. If th_
z___ w_nts Jimmy,
th_y c_n c_m_ _nd
g_t him!"

Beyond the Grave: Ghosts, Ghouls, and Zombies

What did the man in the electric chair ask for?

To have the charges reversed.

Why did the gravedigger keep a pail on the sidewalk?

So someone would kick the bucket.

What's an ax murderer's favorite drink?

Slice.

How do morticians speak?

Gravely.

What's the hardest part about becoming a funeral director?

The stiff competition.

Why did the dead boy stay home from school?

He was feeling rotten.

GROSS-O-METER

In 1999, John Lamedica made the *Guinness Book of World Records* by getting into a coffin with 20,050 giant Madagascan hissing cockroaches. Getting into a coffin when you're not dead and then having 20,050 of anything, let alone giant hissing creatures, crawling all over you gets a ten on the Gross-o-meter scale.

Why couldn't the skeleton fart in a crowded place?

It had no guts.

What did the skeleton buy at the supermarket?

Spare ribs.

Fred: Did you hear about the coffin that just covers the head?

Ed: No, why's that?
Fred: It's for people like you who are dead from the neck up.

What are you supposed to do with an overweight ghost?

Exorcise him.

 77

What do people do as they die?

They bite the dust.

What did the morbid mortician say when he walked into the crematorium?

What's cooking?

Why don't ghosts ever lie?

Because you can see right through them.

Goblin 1: Let's go get some dinner at the graveyard.

Goblin 2: Shall we order out some ribs?

Goblin 1: No, they're always cold by the time we get them home.

Why didn't the skeleton like his job?

His heart wasn't in it.

How do you find a corpse at a zombie family reunion?

The corpse is the one with an expression on his face.

What lies at the bottom of the sea and twitches?

A nervous wreck.

Why don't skeletons play instruments in church?

They have no organs.

Why don't ghouls get up before sunrise?

It never dawned on them.

Why were there long lines at the cemetery?

People were dying to get in.

What did the mummy say when he entered the morgue?

Anybody home?

Why did the man get buried up to his waist?

Because he said he felt half dead.

GROSS-O-METER

Killer seaweed known as caulerpa taxifolia covers thousands of acres of the ocean floor, destroying food for other sea creatures. It's known as a major underwater predator because its slimy clutches grab onto anything it can find. Deadly seaweed gets an eight on the Gross-o-meter scale.

What do you do if you meet a skeleton in a dark alley?

Jump out of your skin and say hello.

Why did the mortician prefer cremations?

It helped him urn more.

Why did the mortician cut up the corpse's nose?

To see what made it run.

Foul Language

Scavenger

Scavengers are animals such as vultures that prey on the already dead. For example, road kill is considerable cause for celebration among scavengers that don't like to work for their dinner.

Grime Time

PUZZLE 1: Find the one time in the letter grid that the word GRIME is spelled correctly. Words can run up, down, diagonally, backward, or forward.

PUZZLE 2: Can you figure out the one letter that is missing from these six words that mean GRIME?

CRD   MD

GNK   DST

MCK   SMDGE

```
G I G G I G R E M I R E
I R M I R G E R G R I G
R G I M G R I G I G R I
I R G M R R I R E R I M
M I G R I M G M I G M E
E M E I M I E M I G I R
G G M G R I E M R M R I
R I E G I E E M I R G G
M M I R G R G E G E M M
E I G R G R I M M I R G
G R E M I M I R I G I E
```

Seriously Sick

Did you ever wonder why dead people are often called stiffs? Well, it's because that's exactly what happens. Soon after someone dies, blood stops circulating and muscles become stiff. This condition is known as rigor mortis. It lasts for about two days until the body begins to relax again.

What do ghouls like on their potatoes?

Grave-y.

What do a corpse and an insect artist have in common?

They both draw flies.

Did you hear about the mummy that ate a light bulb?

He threw it up and now he's delighted.

Why do ghosts scream when someone dies?

The dead are hard of hearing.

Why did the mortician have such a big party?

The morgue the merrier.

Funeral Director: You're sure you want to buy these bodies?

Goblin: Yes, please.
Funeral Director: Shall I wrap them up?
Goblin: No thanks, I'll eat them here.

How do mummies make a phone call?

With a touch-tomb phone.

Rude Rebus Riddles

To solve a rebus puzzle, you must identify each picture, adding or subtracting letters as you read from left to right. The answer will sound correct, but may not be spelled correctly!

HINT: Some words are shown with only one picture—some take more.

What does a cannibal call a man in a hammock?

 **+**

Why don't ghosts ever tell lies?

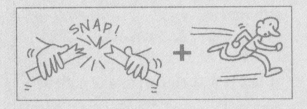 **U**  **M**

Which tiny magical being leaves farts under your pillow?

 **T+**  **F+**

What should a carpenter never hit with a hammer? **A**

What do you call a skeleton who goes around ringing bells?

A dead ringer.

How do you keep a ghoul from biting his nails?

Chop off his hands.

Why did the ghoul eat a light bulb?

He needed a light snack.

Seriously Sick

Did you ever hear of the Black Death? This was a plague that plowed through Europe during the 1300s. It wiped out entire villages, killing about one-third of the European population. Once you got hit with the plague, the only place you were headed was the grave.

How do you keep a dead body from smelling?

Cut off its nose.

Who writes scripts for demon movies?

Crypt writers.

What is a skeleton snake called?

A rattler.

What did the mummy son call his parents?

Mummy and Deady.

Why did the funeral director chop up the corpses?

He wanted them to rest in pieces.

How did the body look after cremation?

Ashen.

What's a skeleton?

Bones with the person scraped off.

Chapter 7

Stinky Stuff

Boyfriend: *What is that perfume you're wearing?*

Girlfriend: *High Heaven.*

Boyfriend: *I asked what perfume it is, not what it stinks to.*

What's long, rotten, and smells of cheese?

Your toenails.

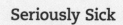

Seriously Sick

The human body has about a quart of gas inside at any one time just bursting to come out. Usually the food you eat causes this. Gas can travel through your body in as little as thirty minutes, but burps come up right away. You burp or fart about fifteen times a day!

Why do so many people hate their noses?

Because they smell.

What did the judge say to the skunk that was on trial?

Odor in the court.

Knock Knock

Who's there?
Consumption.
Consumption who?
Consumption be done about the foul odor in here?

Gross A to Z

Write each of the seven-letter words into the boxes in alphabetical order, starting with the top row and working your way to the bottom. When you're finished, read down the shaded columns to get the answers to these two riddles:

1. **What science fiction movie features a toad?**

2. **What's a fat vampire called?**

RESENDS

BOWLFUL

BARRACK

ANTLERS

OUTWARD

MARINAS

CRACKLE

ABSURDS

AZALEAS

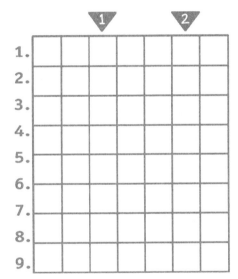

1.
2.
3.
4.
5.
6.
7.
8.
9.

What prize do people get if they cure themselves of body odor?

The no-smell peace prize.

Knock Knock

Who's there?
Philip.
Philip who?
Philip the tub, you stink.

Seriously Sick

Did you ever wonder why dogs sniff each other's rear ends? They have a scent gland right there that helps them recognize one another. Once they know if they're dealing with a dangerous Doberman or a precious poodle, then they can act accordingly.

What do you call a man who smells like fish?

Poor sole.

What do diapers and garbage trucks have in common?

They both hold a smelly load.

Foul Language

Flatulence

This is just a fancy word for farts. When there's too much gas in your digestive tract, you've got flatulence. So if you want to impress someone the next time they fart, just tell them their flatulence is not appreciated. If you've got to talk about farts, why not do it in style?

Knock Knock

Who's there?
Dozen.
Dozen who?
Dozen anybody bathe anymore?
Pew!

What do body odor and peaches have in common?

They both grow around pits.

The Art of Fart

The Tire Fart

This fart is so powerful it sounds like a tire deflating in your pants.

Jail Fart

It's been inside you for some time and you want to let it out. However, you have to wait for the perfect opportunity for it to make its great escape.

Stuck-up Fart

This is when you think your farts don't stink—but they do!

Home Alone Fart

This is when you are home all by yourself so you just let them rip all over the place—loud and free.

Tie Your Shoe Fart

This is when you bend over to tie your shoe laces, and whoops! You let one loose, right in front of Grandma!

The Stainer

This is when you think it's just a fart but it turns out to be a bit more. Now you have to walk around like that all day and hope it dries up.

The Big Bad Fart

This fart makes its presence known in every way possible— with a puff of gas that could blow papers off a desk, a stench so horrible it could kill small animals, and a sound like thunder coming from your pants.

Firing the Missile

This one comes out fast and straight. You don't have much time to aim, but if you're good, you can use your little brother as a target.

The Unidentified Fart

This is when you know you farted, but nobody can prove it was you.

The Stubborn Fart

This fart just won't come out, no matter how badly you want it to. It could take minutes or even hours to release this gassy blast. But when it comes, you feel a lot better.

Knock Knock

Who's there?
Pea.
Pea who?
Pea U, stop farting!

Mrs. Skunk:

Why did you buy so many
boxes of tissues?

Mr. Skunk:

Because I have a stinking cold.

What did the blind skunk do?

He fell in love with a fart.

What do you get when you cross a horse and a skunk?

Whinny the Pew.

What do you call a newborn skunk?

A little stinker.

Why did the fish smell so bad?

Long time no sea.

Knock Knock

Who's there?
Luke.
Luke who?
Luke out, here comes a big fart.

Totally Twisted

There's nothing like smelly feet to prove how gross you are. Follow this advice to really make a stink. Sweat a lot and don't wear any socks. Don't bathe for a week. After that, more than your feet will stink. Rub garlic all over the bottom of your feet to make them extra super-duper smelly. Then show them off to all your friends!

Foul Language

Pus

You know that slimy, oozing stuff that comes out of a cut when it's infected? That's pus. Sometimes it's yellow and sometimes it's green—and it doesn't smell very good. If you've got pus oozing out of any part of your body, it's probably time for a trip to the doctor's office.

What do you get if you cross a skunk and an owl?

A bird that smells but doesn't give a hoot.

Fred: *Did you hear about the man who ate 100 cloves of garlic and then passed out?*
Ed: *No, what happened to him?*
Fred: *The doctor said it was from inhaling his own breath.*

Knock Knock

Who's there?
Jurassic.
Jurassic who?
Jurassic person if you like
these gross jokes.

What goes "Ha, Ha, Ha, PLOP!"

To find out, start at the letter S marked with a dot.

Twist your way over and under, reading every other letter until you get to the end. Then turn around and head back down, reading all the letters you jumped over!

HINT: It helps to cross the letters off as you go.

What do flies and stinky feet have in common?

You can shoe them but they never go away.

How do you keep a pig from smelling?

Plug his nose.

Knock Knock

Who's there?
Sara.
Sara who?
Sara bad smell in the room?

Totally Twisted

Make burping sounds using a balloon, baking soda, vinegar, and a funnel. Using the funnel, pour a quarter of a cup of vinegar in the balloon. Add a tablespoon of baking soda. Squeeze the balloon closed with your fingers. Slowly release your grip, but continue to hold on to the bottom of the balloon. You'll hear a nasty burp.

Gross Garret likes . . .

. . . to pick boogers, but not snot

. . . to sneeze, but not cough

. . . to hiccup, but not burp

. . . to poop, but not fart

. . . to get muddy, but not sticky

. . . to use the bathroom, but not the garage

Can you figure out why Gross Garret likes the things he does?

Do you want to hear some fart jokes?
No, they really stink.

What's invisible and smells like bananas?
Monkey farts.

Knock Knock

Who's there?

Inna

Inna who?

Inna minute there's going to

be a bad smell in here.

Mother: *You have been burping all day!*

Daughter: *It's your fault, you gave me those belchin' waffles for breakfast.*

What kind of book does a skunk like to read?

A best smeller.

Why did the car smell so bad?

It was full of gas.

Totally Twisted

To become an expert farter, start eating fart-inducing foods. Cheese, broccoli, onions, milk, beans, and carbonated beverages are all fart fuel. Another fart tip: If you drink through a straw you'll swallow more air, and chances are you'll get some nice smelly toots.

What smells like a human but isn't a human?

A cannibal fart.

What do burps and kitchens have in common?

They both smell like dinner.

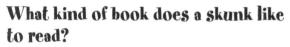

Chapter 8

The Gross-ery Store

Why did the crackers turn green?
They felt crumby.

What kind of meal has both pig parts and human parts?
Pork and beings.

Why did the ham go to the doctor?
It wanted to be cured.

What am I?

I am considered a delicacy by many people around the world. I am made up of cow cheeks or perhaps a pig's nose. Just wrap me up and throw me in a pot for a couple of hours, chill, and then serve on a great big sandwich.
What am I?

Headcheese.

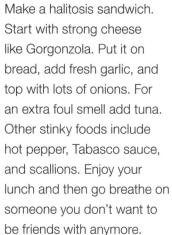

Totally Twisted

Make a halitosis sandwich. Start with strong cheese like Gorgonzola. Put it on bread, add fresh garlic, and top with lots of onions. For an extra foul smell add tuna. Other stinky foods include hot pepper, Tabasco sauce, and scallions. Enjoy your lunch and then go breathe on someone you don't want to be friends with anymore.

Customer: Waiter, why is my pie smushed?
Waiter: Because you said "A slice of cherry pie, and step on it!"

What's sugary on the outside and green on the inside?
A snot-filled donut.

Why did the coffee smell like dirt?
It was just ground.

What do you get from a pampered cow?
Spoiled milk.

What do you eat on your crackers when you're stuck in traffic?

Traffic jam.

Why is food in a monastery so greasy?

It's cooked by friars.

What happens to babies that eat Rice Krispies?

They go snap, crackle, poop.

How did the beans affect Johnny's intestines?

They rectum.

What am I?

I have tentacles that ooze poisonous slippery mucus. I eat nonstop and poop all the time. When I'm frightened I will push my own guts right out of my rear end to ensnare my attacker. If I get really upset I'll shoot thread out of my rear end and lasso my attacker! **What am I?**

A sea cucumber.

What happened to the man who ate too much blue cheese?

He blew chunks.

What happened to the grocery store owner who sat on the meat slicer?

He got behind in his deliveries.

What do you get if you cross a skeleton with peanut butter?

Bones that stick to the roof of your mouth.

Who Foofed?

Someone in this room has accidentally passed some gas. Can you find the path that STARTs at the nose and ENDs at the smelly fellow who needs to say "Excuse me!"

START

END

END

END

The Gross-ery Store

Why are franks and beans good fuel?

Because they provide an endless supply of natural gas.

Is it okay to eat potato chips with your fingers?

No, it's a bad combination.

How do you make a casserole?

Put it on Roller blades.

What's red and green and quivers?

Rotten Jell-O.

What's the most annoying thing about eating pigs-in-a-blanket?

The pigs squeal really loudly when you take a bite.

Seriously Sick
The praying mantis has a pretty sickening diet. Once it chooses its prey, it stabs it with a sharp needle-like appendage. It eats lizards, small birds, and its own babies! Oh, and after the female praying mantis mates, she sometimes likes to eat her partner.

What's worse than eating fresh vomit pie?

Eating two-day-old vomit pie.

What do you get when you cross your dog with an omelet?

Pooched eggs.

Rita: *This gravy is awful.*
Leah: *I made it in my pajamas.*
Rita: *No wonder it's so bad.*

What am I?

You can hold me in your hand and I will slip and slide around. I am made up of water and protein, but I feel like slimy goo. When you think about me, you don't realize how gross I can be until you actually drop me on the floor. It's only when you can't clean me up because I'm so sticky and drippy that you realize how nasty I am. But the truth is, I could have been a baby!
What am I?

An egg yolk.

What's lumpy and green and comes in small containers?
Yogurt gone bad.

What do foot doctors eat for breakfast?
Corn flakes.

What happened to the grape when the ogre sat on it?
It let out a little wine.

How do you make a banana shake?
Sneak up on it and scream.

What do you get if you mix onions and beans?
Tear gas.

What happened to the toddler who ate too much?
He tossed his cookies.

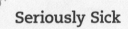

Seriously Sick
Bacteria loves to live on sponges. It loves the grease from your dishes and the wet moistness that the sponge provides. Sponges are the perfect breeding ground for more bacteria. Think about that the next time you're washing dishes with an old sponge.

What's the difference between boogers and Brussels sprouts?

Kids don't eat Brussels sprouts.

What do you call someone who poisons your breakfast?

A cereal killer.

Doctor: Why is your son crying?
Mother: He has baked beans stuck up his nose.
Doctor: Well, why is your daughter crying?
Mother: She wants her lunch back.

Why do people who harvest vegetables have noses?

So they have something to pick during the cold season.

Mrs. Jones: We're having Mother for dinner tomorrow night.

Mr. Jones: Can't we just have hamburgers?

Knock Knock

Who's there?
Eyeball.
Eyeball who?
Eyeball every time I have to eat your food!

What do you call a millionaire with really bad body odor?

To find the answer to this riddle, color in the letters that appear more than two times. Read the remaining letters from left to right and top to bottom.

BOBOFPUBOIBO
PULBOPUBOBO
BOBOBOTBOPU
HPBOBOPUBOY
PUROBOPBOBO
PUIPBOCBOBOH

 99

Customer: *I can't eat this food, it's horrible. Call the chef.*

Waiter: *It's a waste of time, he can't eat it either.*

What do you get if you eat prune pizza?

Pizzeria.

Waiter: *I have boiled liver, cow brains, and chicken feet.*

Customer: *I don't want to hear your medical problems, I just want some lunch.*

Customer: Waiter, waiter!
My dinner is talking to me.

Well, you asked for a tongue sandwich.

What did the pig name his supermarket?

Stop in slop.

Totally Twisted

Quench your thirst with sludge water. You'll need melted chocolate ice cream and something carbonated such as seltzer or cola. Add bits of chocolate or raisins. Prepare this for your friends on a hot day. If they hesitate, offer to try it first.

Seriously Sick

Around the world insects of all kinds are considered tasty treats. In parts of China, people eat de-winged, fried grasshoppers. In parts of South America, biting the head off a live giant ant is the perfect snack. And in the West Indies, roasted grubs make an excellent lunch. Yum!

Why did the blueberry need a lawyer?

It was in a jam.

What's worse than finding a maggot in your cereal?

Finding half a maggot in your cereal.

What's green, brown, and slimy and comes out of your nose?

Chocolate milk after a good joke.

Totally Twisted

Blood pudding is made of real cow or pig blood, so it definitely meets gross factor requirements. To make your own blood pudding, you will need a cup of milk, a teaspoon of sugar, a cup of rice, four cups of cow blood, and a cup of bread crumbs. With an adult's help, mix it all up and bake it for two hours. Mmm.

How do you know when a dumpster is full of toadstools?

There isn't mushroom inside.

What do you call a guy who sells vegetables and throws up all day?

A green grocer.

How can you tell if there are rat pieces in your cookies?

Read the ingredients.

Knock Knock

Who's there?
Pudding.
Pudding who?
Pudding all that chili on your hotdog is going to make you puke.

If a nut on the wall is a walnut, what do you call a nut in the toilet bowl?

A pee can.

What's the difference between roast pork and pea soup?

Anyone can roast pork.

What's red and gooey and found in a shark's mouth?

Slow swimmers.

Knock Knock

Who's there?
Fajita.
Fajita who?
Fajita 'nother bite, I'll be sick.

Totally Twisted

Make edible acne with cherry tomatoes and cream cheese. Have an adult core out the center of the cherry tomatoes and then fill with cream cheese. Once the tomatoes (pimples) are filled, make sure to give them a good squeeze so the pus starts oozing out. Even if you don't have zits on your face, you can still pop these—and then eat them!

Foul Language

Curdle

Did you ever pour some milk in your cereal that had been sitting around a little too long? Not only is there a horrible smell, but the milk isn't even milk anymore, it's just clumps of goop. When something like milk or yogurt goes bad, it's considered curdled.

George: *I just saw a man eating shark!*
Ted: *Where?*
George: *In a restaurant.*

What do you get when you eat a lollipop that has a mosquito on it?

A bloodsucker.

What kind of sandwich do kids hate to take for lunch?

Peanut butter and jellyfish.

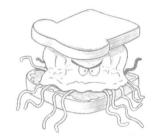

Why did the chef put exactly 239 beans in his pot of chili?

To find the answer to this riddle, drop the letters from each column into the squares directly below them. Careful—the letters won't always be in the same order! Black squares are the spaces between words.

	I	C	E								
	F	A	K	U	W	E			D		
M	M	R	A	T	Y	I	U	O	T	O	
B	O	A	R	E	S	O	T	L	N	E	O
	E			U			▓				
		R		▓	W			D			
▓											
▓		R		!							

Chapter 9

Gooey Games and Sickening Sports

What position did the pig play in football?

Swinebacker.

What happens when a football player kicks a duck?

He foots the bill.

What is an insect's favorite game?

Cricket.

Why don't centipedes play football?

By the time they get their shoes on, the game is over.

Totally Twisted

To have a relay race with egg yolks, separate a group of friends into teams of three. Make sure each team member is standing a good distance away. The first person on each team gets a nice gooey egg yolk on a spoon. The goal is to pass the egg yolk to your teammates without breaking it. Whichever team gets to the finish line with the most yolk wins.

GROSS-O-METER

In 1998, thousands of black money spiders gathered on a ball field in England and created the largest spider web ever reported. It covered over eleven acres. Showing up to soccer practice and getting caught in a humongous sticky, nasty spider web ranks a solid eight on the Gross-o-meter scale.

Why is it so hard to get a job as a sword fighter?

The competition is very cutthroat.

How do you know if a fly is a great American football player?

He's in the sugar bowl.

What kind of competition do mosquitoes like?

Skin diving.

Why did the fans bring toilet paper to the baseball game?

The bases were loaded.

Where's Walmo?

Can you find Walmo by using this description?

- Food in teeth
- White shirt with dark stain
- Dark jeans with light stain
- 3 zits

Totally Twisted

To put together a gross scavenger hunt, make a list of the nasty things that lurk around your house and garden. For example, rotting fruit from the garbage, spider webs, slugs, worms, and dustballs. Gather your friends and start the hunt. The winner is the first to find all the items on the list.

What do vampires eat at a baseball game?

Fangfurters.

What do you call the head roach of a football team?

The roach coach.

What game do zombies play in the schoolyard?

Swallow the leader.

Do you remember when you lost your first tooth?

Yeah, I couldn't believe my brother could kick a football so well.

What was everybody's favorite game show at the leper colony?

Leperdy.

Totally Twisted

Drink a lot of carbonated beverages through a straw so you get real gassy. Your mission is to burp the entire alphabet—backwards. You'll have to practice a lot. Don't be discouraged if you only get up to S the first time around. Just try again, no matter how annoying people tell you you're being.

Name That Poop

Phantom Poop

This is when you think you have to poop, and you try really hard to poop, but no poop comes out.

The No Evidence Poop

This is when you poop a huge poop and you see it, but there's nothing on the toilet paper to prove it.

Sloppy Poop

This is when you wipe and wipe and the poop just won't go away. So, you have to either take a shower or just keep toilet paper in your pants till it dries up.

I'd Give My Kingdom for a Poop

This is when you have to go so badly that you throw your sister to the floor to stop her from going into the bathroom before you. But once you're seated, you just can't poop!

This is probably the worst kind of poop there is.

The Fake-Out Poop

This is when you think you're done pooping so you wipe and flush, but then you realize you still have more poop in you. Only now, your whole family is waiting by the door to get into the bathroom, so you have to hurry.

The Fart Poop

This is when you poop and fart at the same time, and it stinks so bad you can't even breathe. Everyone can hear you poop, too.

The Turtle Poop

This is when you're trying to poop and it comes out a little and then goes right back inside. It takes a couple of tries to finally get it out.

Name That Poop (Continued)

The Watermelon Poop

This poop doesn't smell like watermelon, but rather it feels like one! It feels like the biggest poop of your life and you wonder how in the world it's going to come out of your body. When it finally comes out, you're ready for a nap.

The Dump Truck Poop

This is when you've been holding it for so long that when it finally comes out, your whole rear end gets a giant splash from the force of the poop.

The Curly Poop

This poop is so long that it actually coils up inside the toilet bowl. If it weren't so gross, you'd want to show your friends just how long this poop really is.

Why do frogs join baseball teams?

They catch all the pop flies.

What kind of ball should you never play baseball with?

An eyeball.

What do you call a snowman with a suntan?

A puddle.

How did the ghosts win their football game?

They kicked a field ghoul.

How are shoes similar to a losing football team?

They hate to suffer defeat.

Totally Twisted

Play the putrid picnic game! Gather a group of friends and go around the circle naming gross things you might bring to a putrid picnic in alphabetical order. For example, if your letter is M, you can say, "I'm bringing moldy mushrooms." Keep going around the circle until you've completed the whole alphabet.

What's the best puzzle for someone with zits?

To find the answer to this riddle, think of a word that best fits each of the descriptions. Write the words on the numbered lines, and then transfer each letter into the numbered grid.

1A	2D	3B	4C	5B	6B	7B
		8D	9A	10A		
		11D	12C	13A	14A	

A. Place for pirate gold

‾ ‾ ‾ ‾ ‾
1 9 10 14 13

B. One penny

‾ ‾ ‾ ‾
6 5 3 7

C. Opposite of OFF

‾ ‾
12 4

D. Small round spot

‾ ‾ ‾
11 2 8

Totally Twisted

You can make your own edible barf. All you'll need is a cup of oatmeal, chocolate cocoa powder, and applesauce. Mix together in a pot until it bubbles, but don't let it burn. If you want vomit with chunks, throw in some dried pineapple. Then show your friends how you eat your own "vomit."

Knock Knock

Who's there?
Jamaica.
Jamaica who?
Jamaica mud pie today?

Hide the Gross Stuff

Can you underline the seven gross words hiding in these sentences?
The words you're looking for are in the list, but careful—there are a few extras!

1. "I hope Ellen likes spiders and worms!"

2. Fred's note was far too gross to read.

3. At the zoo, zebras were burping up lunch.

4. Said Mr. Plopp, "I'm pleased to poop!"

5. This lime color is a yucky label choice.

FART
SNORT
BELCH
SNOT
OOZE
GREASE
PEE
SLIME
WAX
PIMPLE
EEL

Chapter 10

Tales of the Gross and Famous

What am I?

I am famous for my strange parenting methods. I lay eggs, and after the father comes along to fertilize the eggs, I make sure to swallow every single one of them to keep them safe. When they hatch, I throw up the slimy babies. **What am I?**

An Australian brooding frog.

What's green and smells?

The Incredible Hulk's fart.

What do you get when you cross a dinosaur and a pig?

Jurassic Pork.

How come Cinderella never made the football team?

She kept running away from the ball.

What's the most important thing Santa tells his reindeer?

Don't eat yellow snow.

What do you get if you cross a science fiction movie with a frog?

Star Warts.

Why does Tigger smell so bad?

Because he plays with Pooh.

What were Tarzan's last words?

Who greased this vine?

Dodging Dog Doo

A practical joker has covered this yard with dog doo—but only some of it is fake! Can you get from the top to the bottom of the yard without smooshing your shoe in the real doo? Put an X through each letter that appears more than three times. The piles that are left are perfectly plastic and safe to walk on.

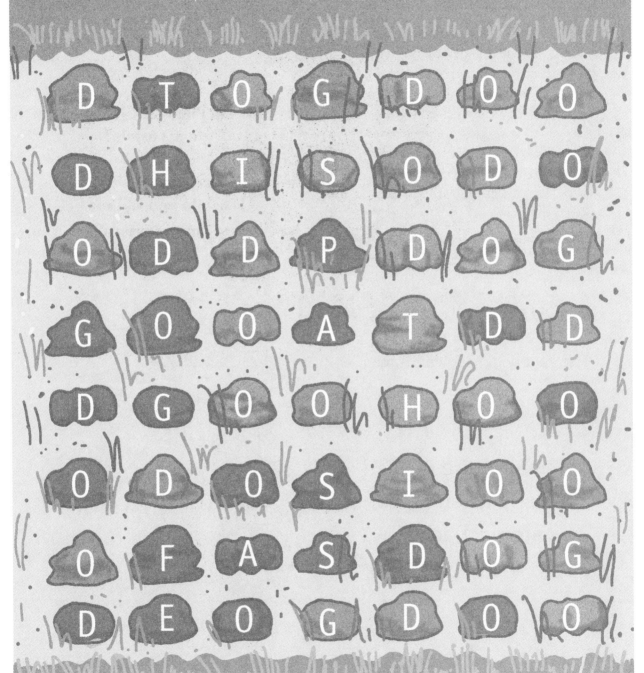

D T O G D O O
D H I S O D O
O D D P D O G
G O O A T D D
D G O O H O O
O D O S I O O
O F A S D O G
D E O G D O O

GROSS-O-METER

In 1998, Kevin Cole of New Mexico broke a world record by ejecting a 7.5 inch strand of spaghetti out of his nostrils. Then he nose-flossed by shooting one end of the spaghetti out of each nostril. Nose flossing gets a sticky nine on the Gross-o-meter scale. Spaghetti and snotballs, anyone?

What do you get if you cross a guillotine with a cowboy who has a sore throat?

A headless hoarse man.

How did Pinocchio get splinters in his hands?

He was scratching his head.

What do you call a large, dancing gorilla?

King Conga.

Why did Frankenstein always get sick after a meal?

He kept bolting down his food.

What did the Big Bad Wolf say when he got a stomachache?

Maybe it was someone I ate.

How did Captain Hook meet his end?

He picked his nose with the wrong hand.

GROSS-O-METER

In 1991, a woman in California made the *Guinness Book of World Records* when her toenails reached over six inches long each. Her husband gave her a choice, him or the toenails. She chose the toenails. Six-inch toenails rank a nasty seven on the Gross-o-meter scale.

What do you call a pig that can climb the side of a building?

Spider ham.

What do you get if you cross a whale with a dead fish?

Moby Ick.

Why did Captain Kirk pee on the ceiling?

To go where no man had gone before.

How do you keep a really gross kid in suspense?

Break the letter code to find the answer to this riddle. **HINT:** Read the answer from top to bottom.

Z − 1	G + 2	V − 2
L + 3	Q − 3	N + 1
V − 1	E − 1	L + 1
'		N − 1
O − 3	P − 1	T − 5
I + 3	P + 5	Q + 1
	U − 1	M + 2
A + 5		Z − 3

What would George Washington do if he were alive today?

Scratch at the lid of his coffin.

What's brown and sits on a piano bench?

Beethoven's last movement.

Why did the Beatles break up?

They were bugging each other.

GROSS-O-METER

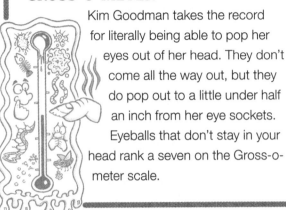

Kim Goodman takes the record for literally being able to pop her eyes out of her head. They don't come all the way out, but they do pop out to a little under half an inch from her eye sockets. Eyeballs that don't stay in your head rank a seven on the Gross-o-meter scale.

Why couldn't Batman go fishing?
Robin ate all the worms.

What do you call Batman after he's been run over by a truck?
Splatman.

GROSS-O-METER

The record for eating the most worms goes to a man in India nicknamed Snake Manu. He ate 200 earthworms in thirty seconds. Eating creepy crawly things gets a nine on the Gross-o-meter scale, but eating them really fast gets a ten.

Knock Knock
Who's there?
Yoda.
Yoda who?
Yoda scariest thing
I've ever seen.

What do you call a booger that's been sneezed across the room?

To find the answer to this riddle, color in all the shapes with the letters S-N-E-E-Z-E.

Why did the Wicked Witch eat turkey?

Flying monkeys are too hard to catch on her broom.

What's the real reason Rudolph has a red nose?

Prancer beat him during a boxing match.

Why do cannibals love Wheel of Fortune?

They like to buy bowels.

Why did Dracula always have breath mints with him?

He suffered from bat breath.

What do you get if you cross Godzilla with a parrot?

A messy cage.

What do you get when you cross a serial killer with a pair of jeans?

Jack the zipper.

Who's green, has a lot of hair, and lives in a tower?

A barfing Rapunzel.

How do you know if the Hunchback of Notre Dame is upset with you?

He gets bent out of shape.

Which barbarian ate the Roman Empire?

Attila the Hungry.

What is Mozart doing now that he's dead?

Decomposing.

What do a spaceship and toilet paper have in common?

They both circle Uranus.

How did the Wicked Witch make yogurt?

She stared at a glass of milk until it curdled.

What do you get when you cross an ant and a rabbit?

Bugs Bunny.

What do you call termites that want to chew up the whole world?

Terminators.

Appendix A: More Books to Read

Branzei, Sylvia. *Grossology and You*. Price, Stern, Sloan. 2002.
This book is so much fun to read you won't realize how much you've actually learned. Great topics of interest such as farting, burping, toe cheese, and more are all part of this adventure into grossness.

Branzei, Sylvia. *Animal Grossology*. Planet Dexter Books. 1996.
If you want to know everything that's gross about animals, this is the book for you. All you'll ever need to know about ticks, leeches, tapeworms, slugs, flies, and even humans is right here.

Chatterton, Martin. *Yuck! The Grossest Joke Book Ever.* **Kingfisher. 2004.**
Over 100 foul and smelly jokes to make you sick and keep you giggling for hours.

Masoff, Joy. *Oh, Yuck! The Encyclopedia of Everything Nasty.* **Workman Publishing. 2000.**
Anything you would ever want to know about the world of the gross and nasty from acne to worms. Includes recipes, experiments, and lots of yucky photos. If you have a passion for the pukey, this will keep you engrossed for hours!

Pellowski, Michael. *Monster Jokes.* **Sterling. 2002.**
Frankenstein, Dracula, and all the werewolves come together in this book for a scary good time. A real chuckler!

Philips, Louis. *Invisible Oink: Pig Jokes.* **Viking Press. 1993.**
Get your fill of oinks and snorts with these hilarious pig jokes. After reading this book you'll surely want to have your very own pig sty.

Solheim, James. *It's Disgusting and We Ate It: True Facts from Around the World and Throughout History.* **Aladdin. 2001.**
Care for some squirrel pie? This book will take you on one of your grossest journeys yet. Travel through history and learn about the totally nasty things people used to eat. Roasted spiders, anyone?

Spoon, Ben. *Gross Jokes and Awesome Body Tricks.* **Element Books. 2000.**

This book will provide hours of fun! Between the jokes and the weird but cool tricks, you can keep your friends laughing for hours.

Stine, Jovial Bob. *101 Creepy Creature Jokes.* **Scholastic. 1997.**

If slimy, stinky creatures are your thing, this book is for you. Sure to leave you rolling with laughter, these jokes are some of the creepiest out there.

Strasser, Todd. *Kid's Book of Gross Facts and Feats.* **Troll Communications. 1998.**

Filled with really gross facts about the human body and amazing but gross things that people have accomplished, this book will satisfy anybody's curiosity about over-the-top grossness.

Szpirglas, Jeff. *Gross Universe: Your Guide to All Things Disgusting under the Sun.* **Maple Tree Press. 2004.**

This book will give you the lowdown on everything from farts to phlegm. You'll learn more about scabs, maggots, and mites than you ever imagined possible.

Appendix B: Web Sites

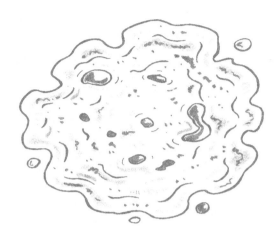

www.ahajokes.com
Amuse friends and family with the jokes on this Web site. Search by category for sick jokes, animal jokes, and much, much more.

www.grossology.org
This Web site discusses the science of everything gross. It focuses on your very stinky, crusty, and slimy body.

http://yucky.kids.discovery.com/noflash/body/index.html
This Web site will tell you all you ever wanted to know about how gross and disgusting your very own body really is. If you're dying to know why people vomit and how come your poop smells so bad, check out this site for all the answers.

http://kidhumor.glowport.com/animal_humor
You'll find tons of jokes about all sorts of animals, including creepy insects such as ants, spiders, fleas, and worms. This Web site will keep you laughing for hours.

www.kidsjokes.co.uk
Search this Web site for hours and you'll be laughing so hard you won't be able to stand up. This site offers all sorts of funnies, including some really gross ones about monsters and creepy crawlers.

http://www.jokesnjokes.net/funny.jokes.amusing.humor.laughs/kids.htm
This Web site will leave you in stitches with its great assortment of one-liners.

http://www.investigator.org.au/funStuff/grossOut.htm
This Web site offers some really cool and extremely gross facts about the human body. Check it out!

http://www.lsc.org/online_science/gross/gross_urinary.html
This official Web site from the Liberty Science Center answers all sorts of questions, such as why your pee smells so bad after you eat asparagus. It also provides a really yummy recipe for making some homemade snot.

http://library.thinkquest.org/03oct/00122/gross.htm
This Web site will totally gross you out with facts about antiquated medical practices. Did you know doctors used to cover sick people in slimy leeches in an effort to suck the disease out of their blood? Check the site to learn more!

http://www.squiglysplayhouse.com/JokesAndRiddles/index.html
This hysterical Web site contains jokes sent in by kids from around the world. It just goes to show you that humor is universal.

Puzzle Answers

page 4 • **Yummy!**

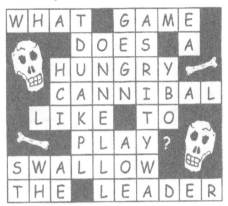

WHAT GAME DOES A HUNGRY CANNIBAL LIKE TO PLAY? SWALLOW THE LEADER

page 7 • **Stink Pinks**

What's a large vehicle
that hauls garbage?
Y U C K   T R U C K

Where can you buy plastic
scars and fake blood?
G O R E   S T O R E

What do you call a shovel
used to pick up dog doo?
P O O P   S C O O P

What do you call
ghost throw up?
S P O O K   P U K E

What do you call
an intelligent gas?
S M A R T   F A R T

What's a riddle
about a dead frog?
C R O A K   J O K E

page 11 • **How do toilets keep in touch?**

page 15 • **What do you get if an ax falls on your head?**

A. Top on a jar
   L I D
   4 5 14

B. Dracula's coat
   C A P E
   16 13 3 12

C. It makes you warm
   H E A T
   11 18 15 7

D. Kids' running game
   T A G
   6 1 10

E. Between knee and ankle
   S H I N
   2 17 8 9

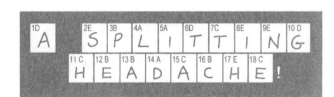

A SPLITTING HEADACHE!

The EVERYTHING KIDS' Gross Jokes Book

page 17 • **What's invisible and smells like bananas?**

M **F**
O **A**
N **R**
K **T**
E **S**
Y

page 20 • Knock, Knock

RIABRIBERIYIRI
ARBRBREYWIHIOR
RABRBERYSTRUZNG
MIEIONMYIBUTIRT

ABBEY. ABBEY WHO?
ABBEY (a bee) STUNG
ME ON MY BUTT!

page 24 • Why couldn't the caveman hear the pterodactyl go to the bathroom?

4 (silent)	3 loudly	1 only
1 cavemen	1 poop!	2 Hear
3 too	3 The	4 (pterodactyls)
4 (have)	1 Because	3 was
3 wooly	4 ("p"!)	1 can
1 hear	3 burping	3 mammoth
4 (a)	2 what?	4 (Because)

Because pterodactyls
have a silent "p"!

page 26 • What do you get if you cross a piranha with your nose?

R wlm'g pmld,
I don't know,
yfg R dlfowm'g
but I wouldn't
dzmg gl krxp rg!
want to pick it!

page 29 • "Your brother sure is spoiled!"

NO**PH**P**ES**P**NO**P
TU**PH**U**P**U**EA**P**LW**
AU**PY**P**S**P**S**P**ME**P
PL**UL**U**PP**P**S**P**T**P**H**
PUAT**PU**W**PAP**Y**P

No he's not. He always smells that way!

page 36 • Snot Milk?

page 41 • Sick Change

Change a small wagon to smelly gas	*Change a flat piece of wood to a crusty wound cover*
CART to FART	**SLAB to SCAB**
Change a tangle of string to a booger	*Change the center of a peach to a pimple*
KNOT to SNOT	**PIT to ZIT**
Change a swollen spot to a belch	*Change a large ring made of metal to a pile of #2*
BUMP to BURP	**HOOP to POOP**

page 46 • What do you call a fairy that never showers?

S	T	I	N	K	E	R	B	E	L	L

page 56 • Sluuuurp

page 56 • Strange Soup

SCORPION SOUP
BIRD NEST SOUP
SHARK FIN SOUP
OXTAIL SOUP

page 60 • On what day of the week do lions eat people?

1. C R U N C H
2. C H O M P
3. M E A T
4. G N A W
5. F E A S T
6. D I N E R
7. S W A L L O W
8. S L O P P Y

page 66 • B-ughs!

1. There are six roaches, but only five spiders. 2. There are six flies. If each fly has six legs, that makes 36 fly legs in all. 3. The mosquito that has just bitten someone is on the left-hand side of the page, near the bottom, between the two flies. You can tell it just had lunch because its belly is swollen with all the blood it just sucked up. Gross!

page 76 • What About Jimmy?

What happened when Jimmy's mother said she was going to take Jimmy to the zoo?

Jimmy's brother said "Don't bother. If the zoo wants Jimmy, they can come and get him!"

page 79 • Grime Time

```
G I G G I G R E M I R E
I R M I R G E R G R I G
R G I M G R I G I G R I
I R G M R R I R E R I M
M I G R I M G M I G M E
E M E I M I E M I G I R
G G M G R I E M R M R I
R I E G I E E M I R G G
M M I R G R G E G E M M
E I G R G R I M M I R G
G R E M I M I R I G I E
```

CRUD   MUD
GUNK   DUST
MUCK   SMUDGE

The missing letter is "U".

page 81 • Rude Rebus Riddles

BREAKFAST   IN   BED

BECAUSE YOU CAN SEE RIGHT THREW 'EM

THE   TOOT   FAIRY

A   FINGERNAIL

A

page 85 • Gross A to Z

A	B	S	U	R	D	S
A	N	T	L	E	R	S
A	Z	A	L	E	A	S
B	A	R	R	A	C	K
B	O	W	L	F	U	L
C	R	A	C	K	L	E
M	A	R	I	N	A	S
O	U	T	W	A	R	D
R	E	S	E	N	D	S

page 89 • What goes "HA, HA, HA, PLOP!"

SOMEONE LAUGHING HIS HEAD OFF!

page 90 • Gross Garret likes . . .

Gross Garret likes anything spelled with double letters!

page 96 • Who Foofed?

page 99 • What do you call a millionaire with really bad body odor?

BOBOFPUBOIBO
PULBOPUBOBO
BOBOBOTBOPU
HPBOBOPUBOY
PUROBOPBOBO
PUIPBOCBOBOH

Answer: FILTHY RICH!

page 102 • Why did the chef put exactly 239 beans in his pot of chili?

	E	C	E							
	F	A	K	U	W	E			D	
M	M	R	A	T	Y	I	U	O	T	O
B	O	A	R	E	S	O	T	L	N	E	O
B	E	C	A	U	S	E		O	N	E
M	O	R	E		W	O	U	L	D	
	M	A	K	E		I	T		T	O	O
	F	A	R	T	Y	! (240- get it?)

page 105 • Where's Walmo?

page 109 • What's the best puzzle for someone with zits?

A. Place for pirate gold

$$\underline{C}\ \underline{H}\ \underline{E}\ \underline{S}\ \underline{T}$$
1 9 10 14 13

B. One penny

$$\underline{C}\ \underline{E}\ \underline{N}\ \underline{T}$$
6 5 3 7

C. Opposite of OFF

$$\underline{O}\ \underline{N}$$
12 4

D. Small round spot

$$\underline{D}\ \underline{O}\ \underline{T}$$
11 2 8

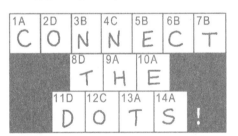

1A	2D	3B	4C	5B	6B	7B
C	O	N	N	E	C	T

8D	9A	10A
T	H	E

11D	12C	13A	14A
D	O	T	S	!

page 110 • Hide the Gross Stuff

1. "I h<u>ope</u> <u>Ellen</u> likes spiders and worms!"

2. Fred's <u>note</u> was <u>far</u> <u>too</u> gross to read.

3. At the <u>zoo</u>, <u>zebras</u> were burping up lunch.

4. Said Mr. Plopp, "I'm <u>pleased</u> to poop!"

5. This <u>lime</u> color is a yucky <u>label</u> choice.

page 113 • Dodging Dog Doo

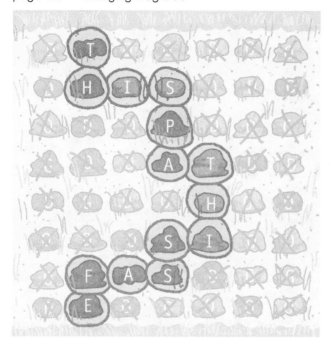

page 116 • How do you keep a really gross kid in suspense?

Z-1 Y	G+2 I	V-2 T
L+3 O	Q-3 N	N+1 O
V-1 U	E-1 D	L+1 M
I		N-1 M
O-3 L	P-1 O	T-5 O
I+3 L	P+5 U	Q+1 R
	U-1 T	M+2 O
A+5 F		Z-3 W

page 118 • What do you call a booger that's been sneezed across the room?

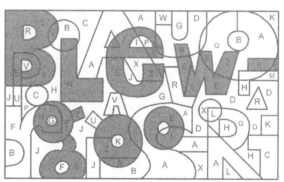

The Everything® KIDS' Series!

Packed with tons of information, activities, and puzzles, the Everything® Kids' books are perennial bestsellers that keep kids active and engaged.

Each book is two-color, 8" x 9¼", and 144 pages.

All this at the incredible price of $6.95!

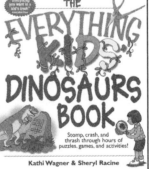

The Everything® Kids' Crazy
Puzzles Book
1-59337-361-9

The Everything® Kids'
Dinosaurs Book
1-59337-360-0

A silly, goofy, and undeniably icky addition to
the Everything® Kids' series . . .

The Everything® Kids'
GROSS
Series

Chock-full of sickening entertainment for hours of disgusting fun.

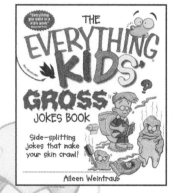

The Everything® Kids' Gross
Jokes Book
1-59337-448-8

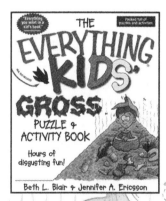

The Everything® Kids' Gross
Puzzle & Activity Book
1-59337-447-X

Other Everything® Kids' Titles Available

The Everything® Kids' Animal Puzzle & Activity Book
1-59337-305-8

The Everything® Kids' Baseball Book, 3rd Ed.
1-59337-070-9

The Everything® Kids' Bible Trivia Book
1-59337-031-8

The Everything® Kids' Bugs Book
1-58062-892-3

The Everything® Kids' Christmas Puzzle & Activity Book
1-58062-965-2

The Everything® Kids' Cookbook
1-58062-658-0

The Everything® Kids' Halloween Puzzle & Activity Book .
1-58062-959-8

The Everything® Kids' Hidden Pictures Book
1-59337-128-4

The Everything® Kids' Joke Book
1-58062-686-6

The Everything® Kids' Knock Knock Book
1-59337-127-6

The Everything® Kids' Math Puzzles Book
1-58062-773-0

The Everything® Kids' Mazes Book
1-58062-558-4

The Everything® Kids' Money Book
1-58062-685-8

The Everything® Kids' Nature Book
1-58062-684-X

The Everything® Kids' Puzzle Book
1-58062-687-4

The Everything® Kids' Riddles & Brain Teasers Book
1-59337-036-9

The Everything® Kids' Science Experiments Book
1-58062-557-6

The Everything® Kids' Sharks Book
1-59337-304-X

The Everything® Kids' Soccer Book
1-58062-642-4

The Everything® Kids' Travel Activity Book
1-58062-641-6

Available wherever books are sold!
To order, call 800-258-0929, or visit us at www.everything.com
Everything® and everything.com® are registered trademarks of F+W Publications, Inc..